PLAYING DEAD

Also by Rudy Wiebe

FICTION

My Lovely Enemy

The Angel of the Tar Sands

The Mad Trapper

Alberta / A Celebration
(with Harry Savage and Tom Radford)

The Scorched-Wood People

Where is the Voice Coming From?

The Temptations of Big Bear

The Blue Mountains of China

First and Vital Candle

Peace Shall Destroy Many

OTHER PROSE

War in the West
(with Bob Beal)

A Voice in the Land
(edited by W.J. Keith)

DRAMA

Far as the Eye Can See
(with Theatre Passe Muraille)

PLAYING DEAD

A contemplation concerning the Arctic

Rudy Wiebe

NeWest

First edition

Canadian Cataloguing in Publication Data

Wiebe, Rudy, 1934-
  Playing dead

ISBN 0-920897-63-0 (bound). — ISBN 0-920897-61-4 (pbk.)

1. Arctic regions - Description and travel. 2. Arctic regions - History. 3. Canada, Northern - Description and travel. 4. Canada, Northern - History. 5. Inuit - Canada.* 6. Indians of North America - Canada, Northern. I. Title.
FC3956.W54   1989   971.9'03   C89-091174-6   F1090.5.W54   1989

Credits

Cover & Interior design: Marna Bunnell
Map: Mostly Maps, Edmonton
Author photograph: Harry Savage
Editor for the Press: Smaro Kamboureli
Printing and binding: Hignell Printing Limited, Manitoba
Financial assistance: Alberta Culture, The Alberta Foundation for the Literary Arts, The Canada Council

Printed and Bound in Canada

NeWest Publishers Limited
Suite 310, 10359 - 82 Avenue
Edmonton, AB, T6E 1Z9

Acknowledgements & Permissions

The publisher and author gratefully acknowledge the following for permission to reprint quoted material:

From I.S. MacLaren and John Franklin in *Profiles in Canadian Literature*, Volume 5 (Toronto: Dundurn Press, 1986).
From Anthony Apakark Thrasher, *Thrasher . . . Skid Row Eskimo* (Toronto: Griffin House, 1976).
From Agnes Nanogak, *More Tales from the Igloo* (Edmonton: Hurtig Publishers Ltd., 1986).
From *People From Our Side*, An Inuit Life Story with Photographs by Peter Pitseolak and Oral Biography by Dorothy Eber (Edmonton: Hurtig Publishers Ltd., and Indiana University Press, 1975).
From Robert Hood, *To the Arctic by Canoe, 1819-1821 / The Journal and Paintings of Robert Hood*. Editor C. Stuart Houston (Montreal and London: McGill-Queen's University Press, 1974).
From John Richardson, *Arctic Ordeal / The Journal of John Richardson, 1820-1822*. Editor C. Stuart Houston (Montreal and London: McGill-Queen's University Press, 1974).
From Hugh MacLennan, *Seven Rivers of Canada*, (Toronto: Macmillan, 1961).
From *The Portable Chekhov*, translated by Avrahm Yarmolinsky. Copyright 1947 by The Viking Press, Inc. Copyright renewed © 1975 by Avrahm Yarmolinsky. All rights reserved. Reprinted by permission of Viking Penguin, a division of Penguin Books USA, Inc.
From Robert Kroetsch, *But We Are Exiles*, (Toronto: Macmillan, 1965). By permission of the author.

Every effort has been made to obtain permission for quoted material. If there is an omission or error the author and publisher would be grateful to be so informed.

CONTENTS

These essays, in somewhat different form and under the title "The Arctic: Landscape of the Spirit," were first presented as the Larkin-Stuart Lectures at Trinity College, the University of Toronto, on November 3-5, 1987. I want to thank Provost Robert H. Painter for inviting me to prepare them.

Rudy Wiebe

Edmonton, April 1989

KESHARRAH A COPPER INDIAN GUIDE AND HIS DAUGHTER GREEN STOCKINGS.
mending a snow shoe.

Published March 1823 by John Murray London.

for

Michael Steven Wiebe

1961 - 1985

Introduction:

THE ORIGIN OF ICE

It is said that once, long ago, the earth was warm. No clouds, no snow, no ice or fog existed. The sun said, "I know the people all over earth," and in the evening when the moon went down she said, "it's going to be so dark now, those people's eyes will be sticking out of their heads."

In those days animals talked like people. One day a brown bear caught an Inuit named Upaum, knocked him down and dragged him to her den. "Here's something for you to suck," she told her cubs. "I'm tired from all this hunting and I need to rest, so you watch while I sleep and when I wake up I'll make you lunch."

Upaum lay where she had dropped him, eyes closed, pretending to be dead. When the bear began to snore he opened one eye just a little, but the cubs were watching closely and immediately they both cried, "Mother! Mother! He's opening his eyes, he's opening his eyes!" The bear sprang up ready to pounce, but Upaum was lying there as motionless as before, so after a while she went back to sleep again. Upaum lay as if he were dead; not even when the cubs rolled him around the floor and licked him hungrily until he itched all over did he so much as move an eyebrow.

Finally the cubs grew tired of playing with their lunch and went out to get more firewood. When all was quiet the man said to himself, "Upaum, now is the time to open your eyes and do something." A broken piece of driftwood lay by the firepit. He stood up silently, seized the wood and hit the bear on the head as hard as he could. For a moment she lay stunned, and Upaum ran for his life.

But the next moment she was coming after him, roaring dreadfully. He knew he could not outrun her so he climbed to the top of some willows and clung there pretending to be a branch while the bear searched all around on the ground below. He said to himself, "As long as the sun shines, I can hang on without getting tired," but he could not hold on that long. He had to come down and run again, and of course the bear found his trail and was after him at once.

Upaum was running north and as he ran he bent down and drew a line with his finger in the earth. Immediately a great stream of water gushed along the line, growing into a huge river that flowed between him and the bear. She stopped on the bank and called to him, "How did you get across this big river?" Upaum called back, "I drank it and snuffled it up so it was empty."

So of course the bear tried to do the same. She drank and drank but she could not empty the river. She drank until finally she burst. The water from her warm body turned into mist and rose, steaming into the sky. For a time Upaum was lost in this fog, but finally it drifted upward and he could find his way home again. This is how fog, and clouds, and

4

rain came to be, and the great river flowing north to the sea became the Coppermine. When cold and dark followed the clouds, the rain became snow and the water ice. That is why the world is the way it is.

As told by Ikpakhuaq and Uloqsaq, Copper Inuit, 1913-16

I

EXERCISING REFLECTION

Here the interminable
ends: here
all things begin:
the river's farewell in the ice,
the marriage of air and the snow.

Pablo Neruda, "Stones of Antarctica", 1961

After twenty-five years of flying over Canada, I began to understand that a human being is a creature of land and air. I have stared down at my country for hundreds of hours as it spreads out below me like a map. Implausibly it lies there, etched in sunlight or patterned by numberless night lights moving on highways and fixed in farmyards and towns and the cross-hatch of city streets, or hidden between, behind and through clouds. And gradually I have become convinced that the only natural human boundary is water.

The Great Lakes are there, yes, and the brief Niagara River, but so much of Canada's southern boundary is invisible from the air; too much of its southern edge was conceived in the imagination of officials who had never and had never intended to see it. Whatever that southern boundary is, it was apparently discovered among the movements of heavenly bodies, translated to earth by means of instruments and remains invisible even from the air to a normal human eye. I have flown across that surmised edge often by day or night, and neither the sun nor sundogs nor the light of the moon and stars or even the aurora borealis granted it the faintest visibility. They never will. And it has come to me that so much of what makes Canada geographically artificial as the nation of the northern half of North America is exactly that: its lack of definition by water.

There is no such lack in the Arctic. Flying north to Herschel Island or Tuktoyaktuk or Paulatuk, the limits of Canada are clear and definite even under ice; and when you stand on the sand of Darnley Bay or on the ice ridge pressured up the beach at Kittigazuit, the boundary of Canada is nothing if not absolute. There, straight along the constellation of the Great Bear (Arctus) past the rim of Banks Island across the permanent Polar Ice is the North Pole (also invisible) and Novaya Zemlya and eventually Siberia, about whose northern edge there is nor ever has been any question whatever. The water declares it. But when you stand on the edge of Canada at the Arctic Ocean and look around, what is not clear is where that ocean begins and the Mackenzie or Hornaday Rivers (you might add any number of other rivers: the Peel, the Anderson, the Horton, the Rae, the Coppermine, the Hood, the Burnside, the Back), where does the ocean begin and where do the rivers end?

The small boat that carried me through fog over the ocean to the Hornaday River compounded my confusion. Edward Ruben, the Mackenzie Inuit owner of the boat, told me we were going to the river, though my eyes told me nothing. Occasionally through fog or water materializing on my glasses I would see dark shoals rising almost to the surface of the grey water; occasionally a darkness which James Ruben, the driver of the boat, said was land shaped itself upward in air. But I saw only angry water, the kind of immediate particularity of long swell and sharp, vicious waves breaking against the thin edge of the boat which chill you very deeply, a "zero at the bone" though you know you are perfectly warm and dry and, apparently, safe. The surface of the shoals we threaded between literally boiled like a swift, frothing mat. Suddenly James cut the high whine of the engine and I heard another motor, and above that the interlaced sound of human voices, and then the fog shifted and a boat was there, filled with people waving, and also a second boat. The sight of them was strangely foreshortened by that deceptive light from the sudden sea. They seemed thrust forward, seemed higher, as if projected above me though clearly they had to be as level with us as anything ever can be on a globe turning in space, and James looked ahead again, guided the boat to the right. "They left before we did," he said, "and got lost — but now we're in the river." The waves and shoals looked the same, the fog which destroyed not only perspective but eliminated all horizon seemed exactly the same; but then a gradual rift of sunlight revealed upthrust land. The water was not salty.

When had we entered the river? Can only taste tell? As Hugh MacLennan asks in his *Seven Rivers of Canada*: "What is a river, anyway?" To answer he considers the Columbia Icefield in the Rocky Mountains on the border between Alberta and British Columbia. This massive remainder of an ice age ten thousand years ago originates streams that move towards three oceans. Though much of these various waters evaporate, MacLennan decides that:

Incredibly, we must presume that some of the water from the Icefield really does go all the way down to the various oceans. [On the other hand] ... the water which evaporates, of course, turns into clouds, and the clouds into rain and snow which may fall as the winds carry them and rejoin other streams quite different from

11

their originals. When Shelley wrote *The Cloud* was he not in a sense writing of rivers? Is it fanciful to imagine that all the rivers of the northern hemisphere, if not of the world, are in this sense interconnected?

The sun and the wind sweep the fog with abrupt swiftness from the cliffs and the wide prospect of the Hornaday River opens, bending south between shoals and water smashing on rocks into the tilted, level tundra. Here it is clear to me that MacLennan's supposition is not fanciful at all. In fact, a further concept is necessary to complete it. I watch the men (there is Edward Ruben, his son James, and his two grandsons) hang over the prow of the boat and lift from the water nets in which arctic char thrash and flicker: the fish make no distinction of borders here. They grow large and fat in the distant reaches of the Arctic Ocean but every August they return up the rivers where they were born — the Hornaday or the Horton or the Back, up the Peel and the Rat, to breed and spawn far inland. But "inland" is a convenient chimera, a mythological beast concocted by our refusal to imagine and thereby to understand. Though we ordinarily think that rivers run from the heights of land and mountains to eventually vanish in the sea, when you approach a river from the ocean it becomes much more enlightening to recognize that rivers are the gnarled fresh fingers of the sea reaching for the mountains.

Below my office window move the waters of the North Saskatchewan River. I can also say that below my window move the waters (running with ice pans now) of that vast inland sea, Hudson Bay. And less than a hundred kilometres north of me on the North Saskatchewan is the Athabasca River which is the water of the Slave River, the Mackenzie River, of the Beaufort Sea, the Arctic Ocean. My city Edmonton began as a fur-trading post in 1795 and the reason it grew to become the dominant northern trading settlement of the nineteenth century is exactly because it is at the closest point between the two water systems: here sixty miles of horse-drawn carts could take you from Hudson Bay to the western Arctic Ocean. The North Saskatchewan and the Athabasca are merely two small (though several thousand kilometres long) tentacles of the Circumpolar Sea, call parts of it what we will — Arctic, North Atlantic, North Pacific, Bering, Beaufort, Chukchi, East Siberian — whatever, that great global sea which surrounds us and in so doing defines our true boundaries.

For some time science has tried to explain the continuum of life to us by supposing that somewhere, before imaginable time, certain living organisms crawled onto land out of the sea. If that is so, then it was not geological ignorance but subliminal, primordial wisdom which caused our ancestors to mythologize that all land (the element where human beings now live) floats on water, and to tell creation stories about the eternal waters which lie beneath all and cradle all and sustain all. We believe now that the planet nearest us, Mars, supports no life as we understand it because it has no water; the river below my window which I with delight watch in its changing seasons, this river tells me I live on the edge of the northern sea, that is the living, global sea. When I cross a bridge or walk along or across the smallest frozen stream, anywhere, when I consider clouds or fly through them, I consciously and unconsciously recognize the living continuum of the sea which sustains and defines me.

If then the endless tentacles of the sea lie everywhere on the land, it is both philosophically proper and imaginatively pleasing that the first whites to systematically explore the Canadian Arctic tundra and its coast were sailors.

As early as 1576 the English sailor-cum-pirate Martin Frobisher had encountered the then unnamed Baffin Island, though he stepped onto it only long enough to lose five men and steal one from it in return (is a sailor's land instinct primarily violence and plunder?), but more than two hundred years later the only parts of the Arctic coast west of Hudson Bay known to whites were the mouth (or entrance in my mythology) of the Coppermine River which Samuel Hearne reached by walking overland on July 17, 1771, and the Mackenzie River delta seen by Alexander Mackenzie from a canoe on July 12, 1789. White men did not 'discover' Canada's northern coast in the standard fashion we understand of sailors in ships exploring a shoreline, anchoring and sending out boats to chart bays and possible rivers, returning and then continuing on in the ships. No; in the summer of 1821, when nothing more was known about Canada's western Arctic coast than the two deltas Hearne and Mackenzie had seen as it were for a moment, in 1821, 764.5 miles of Arctic coast was mapped by five English sailors who got there by following river systems across the tundra from the present site of Yellowknife, Northwest Territories, north via Winter Lake and down the Coppermine River to the sea. French Canadian voyageurs paddled them there and then through the ice along the Arctic coast in birchbark canoes. This is of course the first Franklin expedition of 1819-22, led by the same John Franklin who on his third venture to the polar seas in 1845 became world famous when he and his 130 sailors on two ships, one called *Erebus* (son of Chaos, brother of Night) and the other *Terror* (what hellish names, those) vanished forever into arctic space. Most of their bodies have never been discovered. I am not being facetious when I say that on the evidence of his first and second expedition it would have been better for Franklin if he, in a

14

land of moving ice and no trees, had remained with canoes and voyageurs. On his first expedition he destroyed all the canoes and most of the voyageurs but, though it was nip and tuck for a time, four of the five English sailors did survive. Including himself.

In startling contrast to the difficulty even the strongest white men have with living in the Arctic, the Inuit — both men and women, infants and elderly — have lived there happily for at least eight thousand years. They developed a superb technology for clothing themselves, for building shelter, for hunting and for finding each other in an uninhabited and untracked landscape of snow and ice and tundra which for several weeks of each year is in total darkness. But it is the Inuit linguistic concept of spatial dimension which best helps us to understand the relative success of Franklin's first two expeditions and the disaster of his third.

The Inuit express spatial concepts in two fundamental ways. The linguist Raymond Gagné has deduced that in Inuktitut:

all visible phenomena . . . — whether things, beings, places, areas, or surfaces — are viewed two-dimensionally. Moreover, all of them fall into two basic categories: first, those whose visible limits are in fact, or appear to the speaker to be, of roughly equal dimensions, such as a ball, an igloo . . . or an ice surface; and second, those that are or appear to be of unequal dimensions (that is, things that are distinctly longer than they are wide), such as a harpoon, . . . a rope, . . . or a river.

Further: any object normally classified as the first (a ball) changes into the second when in motion (a rolling ball). This second feature of spatial concept the Inuit share with the Indians: when a human being moves he changes from being "areal" to "linear." Thus to travel on a river means to travel doubly linearly: you are moving (single file) along a single path, that provided by the river or by portages between rivers. That was the way the fur traders (Hearne, Mackenzie) and the first two Franklin expeditions explored the land. On the other hand, the Royal British Navy moved quite differently. It became the chief agent of arctic exploration after the defeat of Napoleon confirmed Britain's pride of World Empire in a way it had not experienced since the days of Elizabeth I, a pride which helped the Admiralty decide that its next great project would be the discovery of the Northwest Passage, an exclusive English route to the Orient. Such a discovery would of course build both the territorial and commercial pillars of Empire. And the Royal Navy always moved in terms of both latitude and longitude. That is, in contrast to the linear movement of the fur traders from point to point, sailors accustomed to the fluid, trackless seas moved in terms of area. At the same time they travelled "heavy": in accordance with their concept of "empty" seas which they could traverse in any of the wind's directions in relatively large-capacity vessels, they carried with them from home everything they could possibly imagine they might need. In naval arctic exploration this heaviness always included far more men (there was enormous unemployment in Great Britain after the Napoleonic Wars) than the fragile ecology of the North could of itself sustain, but to their thinking this did not matter since there was always a large shipload of supplies available. Nevertheless it does matter, absolutely, when the "heavy" ship becomes beset by ice (that is, by water pretending to be land and as untraversable by ship as land itself) and is thereby suddenly forced into *motionlessness*. In Inuktitut a different expression is used for the same object when it is moving or motionless: that is, when it is no longer line but area. A ship frozen in the ice has moved out of the linear into another dimension altogether:

in the vast Arctic it has achieved the dimension of areal *stillness*. That is a dimension which sailors, experienced only in the endless, unbounded motion of the sea, cannot understand. Stillness destroys them. In the first decade of Victoria's glorious reign, several years of icy stillness for *Erebus* and *Terror* on the coast of King William Island destroyed Britain's greatest arctic expedition: every man on it died. Most of their skeletons have never been found, neither have the two ships.

Perhaps the implacable ice holds them still. Perhaps in one or another of those endless, gigantic ice pressure ridges shifting, sinking, reshaping themselves forever in the ice streams that flow between the islands of the Canadian archipelago, *Erebus* and *Terror* are still carried, hidden and secret. Their tall masts are long since destroyed and their decks gouged, splintered, walled in by impenetrable floes, the ice a shroud scraping over these great oaken sailing ships of empire, their skeleton crews rigid in a final posture of convulsive movement. They could be anywhere in the Arctic Ocean for the ice flows hundreds of kilometres a year; long separated now, perhaps at intervals the ice opens and one or the other is revealed for a moment or a year, a mast stump or a bowsprit reaching like a hand, briefly, up into the light somewhere off the coast of Ellesmere or Axel Heiberg islands. Or perhaps they have left the Canadian Arctic long ago and the ice has discovered for them the farthest Northwest Passage of all, the circular passage that leads past the New Siberian Islands and between Novaya Zemlya and Franz Josef Land, past West Spitzbergen and north around Greenland and south through Kennedy Channel and then Lancaster Sound once more and down Peel Sound until now, after a century and a half they are about to meet again for a moment at the place of their ultimate, fatal ignorance off the western shore of King William Island. Perhaps then, with the discovery that the earth is always round, that death is always return, the ice will relent; then, beyond the indifferent sun and moon and the unborn Inuit children dancing with their umbilical cords which are the northern lights, then at last a living human being will be allowed to see them and cry, "Here, here!" imagining of course that they have been there always, though hidden; cry, "Here is *Erebus*! Here at last is *Terror*!"

In 1893 the brilliant Norwegian Fridtjof Nansen deliberately planned that his ship, the *Fram*, drift in the circumpolar ice to discover the movement of its floes. Frozen fast in the ice, it drifted for three years and several thousand kilometres. Nansen noted that by the seventeenth and eighteenth centuries the Russians had already "mapped the whole Siberian coast from the borders of Europe to the Bering Strait" and many of their arctic islands by travelling in winter like the natives and using dogsleds. By the middle of the nineteenth century a few English sea captains were making excellent use of Inuit travel methods, complete with snow houses for overnight camping; the discovery of the fate of the third Franklin expedition by Captain Francis M'Clintock and his fellow officers W.R. Hobson and Allen Young (1857-59) would have been impossible without dogs and sleds. Nevertheless the English persisted with summer ships, and when after three hundred years they could no longer ignore the eternal ice and the ten- or eleven-month northern winters, some still held to their particular refusal of Inuit methods: in May 1876, exactly three centuries after Martin Frobisher set sail for Baffin Island, Captain Albert Markham trekked by sled from his ice-bound *Alert* to eighty-three degrees north, beyond the tip of Ellesmere Island which is the second most northerly point of land on the globe. However, despite the fact that there were plenty of dogs on board his ship, Markham used thirty-three sailors to pull his sleds. Nansen remarks wryly, "It would appear, indeed, as if dogs were not held in great estimation by the English." Indeed. In 1911 Roald Amundsen, who had trained under Nansen, reached and returned from the South Pole in relative comfort using dogteams. At the same time, Robert Falcon Scott and his entire English expedition starved and froze to death because they tried to use horses.

If the English were so stubborn about obvious weather and Inuit technology, they could not possibly appreciate the subtleties of Inuit spatial perception as revealed in their language. Historian Hugh Wallace has intimated that the Arctic hid its Franklin secret so well because the Royal Navy did not comprehend, as the Inuit perforce do, the necessary arctic distinctions between linear and areal space. The navy, which had failed to find the linear Northwest Passage when looking for it by areal means, in 1848 began looking for motionless dots (the two Franklin ships) in the most geographically complicated quarter of the Arctic Ocean by areal means as well. But in Inuit terms the problem always remained linear because (to quote Gagné again), "Any area without easily definable limits, such as a wide expanse of land or sea, is automatically classified as of unequal dimensions," that is, as being long and narrow. Therefore, in order to hunt for an animal or a human being in such an expanse you do not move back and forth in a slow areal search; rather, you lay one quick line of tracks across the entire expanse looking for evidence of a line of motion that can lead you to the motionless spot. That is exactly how, on the first Franklin expedition in 1821, the Metis translator Pierre St. Germain led George Back to find on the vast tundra the tiny Indian camp whose food saved the four remaining

Englishmen from death by starvation. The Royal Navy needed over two million pounds sterling and more than twenty vessels sailing over thirty voyages in ten years to wring from the arctic ice the most elementary of Franklin secrets: where did he die? The other more complex secrets surrounding his fate — what? — how? — why? — are still being puzzled over.

Inuit travel technology and their two-dimensional understanding of space, both of which were taught them by the awesome landscape in which they have learned to live, explain perfectly the survival of the first Franklin expedition of 1819-22. Franklin's orders were to map the northern coast of the continent east of the Coppermine River, making exact readings of latitude, longitude, and recording weather, minerals, flora and fauna. No one, least of all the British Admiralty, had the slightest conception of how long a naval expedition would take to get to the mouth of the Copper-mine River by land, which was the only way any white (that is, Samuel Hearne, but he was a solitary fur trader walking with Indians) had ever got there, nor what difficulties the coast would present. However, John Franklin, aged thirty-three, together with medical doctor and naturalist Dr. John Richardson, thirty-one, midshipmen George Back and Robert Hood, both twenty-two, and ordinary seaman John Hepburn, thirty, sail from Gravesend on May 23, 1819, on board the Hudson's Bay Company ship *Prince of Wales* for York Factory to explore that coast. It takes them an extraordinary three months to get into Hudson Bay; they arrive at York Factory on August 29. After a week's preparation they continue their linear quest along the Hayes River and the Saskatchewan, 685 miles to Cumberland House, which they just reach by freeze-up on October 23. They settle for winter: become motionless spots there.

By means of (most unsailorly) snowshoes, Franklin and Back trek ahead while Hood and Dr. Richardson remain at Cumberland House. Young Midshipman Robert Hood is unaccustomed to both the nightly "dismal serenade" of the "cowardly, stupid and ravenous" sled dogs and to the lazy winter lives of the traders, "few of [whom] have books, and the incidents of their lives do not furnish much subject for thought." Hood decides: "In such a state one might be disposed to envy the half year's slumber of the bears." With unconscious wit he is recognizing that a sailor, who has no means of movement in the North when moving water turns motionless (that is, turns from linear to areal), a sailor might well adopt the winter behavior of local animals. That local human beings (despite their blatant lack of books) might also have a great deal to teach him seems to pass him by.

The English officers do, however, make careful scientific notes (including a lengthy description of the local Cree Indians) and Hood especially makes important magnetic readings and paints landscapes, people and animals, besides writing a perceptive, amusing journal much more revealing than the usual explorer diary. And on June 13, 1820, (after nearly eight months of motionlessness) they resume their linear trek up the Churchill, over the Methye Portage, where they leave Hudson Bay water and join those of the Arctic Ocean, paddling down the Clearwater and Athabasca rivers to Fort Chipewyan. They arrive there on July 13. They are following the traditional fur trade route and they have had no problem with their hired voyageurs (except that their head man drowns on a portage, an occupational hazard one assumes) until they reach Fort Providence on the north shore of Great Slave Lake on July 29, well over a thousand river miles from Cumberland House.

It was here that they must leave the regular trade routes to move north and the voyageurs, who will have to literally carry on their backs all the supplies up over the height of land into the Coppermine basin, begin to voice serious doubts. The Yellowknife Indians and their chief Akaitcho agree to hunt for them, and draw maps of a possible route on the ground. They tell them they personally have never traversed the entire route by canoe, but they think the head-waters of the Yellowknife River system can be reached within ten days where they can perhaps cross a lake to the edge of the treeline, which would be a good place to winter. After that it can be another four or five days of river and portage to connect with the Coppermine.

But more than an untravelled route, the voyageurs are concerned with travelling "heavy." Here is Hood's description of their party and supplies:

We gave guns, ammunition, tobacco, blankets and cloth, to the Indians. Our remaining stores were a few unserviceable guns, eight pistols, 24 broad daggers, two barrels of powder, and balls for 2/3 of that quantity, nails and fastenings for a boat, some knives, chisels, files, axes, and a hand saw; six nets, with meshes of different sizes; some cloth, needles, looking glasses, blankets, and beads. Our provision was two barrels of flour, two cases of chocolate, two canisters of tea, 200 dried reindeer tongues, and portable soups, arrowroot, and dried moose meat for ten days. The expedition consisted of 28 persons, including five officers, two interpreters and three Bois brulée women, who were engaged to make shoes and clothes at the winter establishment.

The weight of canoes and cargo is four tons, all to be heaved over the innumerable rocks and portages of the torturous Yellowknife River by eighteen voyageurs. The officers, as befits the hierarchy of the Royal Navy which informed the expedition throughout, carry only their instruments and personal papers while John Hepburn, quite properly for an ordinary English sailor, has to work and sleep with the voyageurs although he can not even converse with them in their particular French Canadian. The party leaves Great Slave Lake on August 2, preceded by a large flotilla of Indian canoes which even on the initial portages quickly outdistances the English because the women and children also help carry. This convinces Hood that the Indians had very much overestimated the expedition's possible speed.

He is correct. By August 5, after six portages on a single day, they have barely progressed and are already down to the spare provisions of "portable soup." Fishing is unsuccessful and the hunters nowhere in sight; by August 12 they are not halfway up the Yellowknife River and the limping voyageurs are giving "up all hope of relief." They threaten to desert and Franklin, like any good English sea captain, "denounc[ed] the heaviest punishment against the ringleaders."

It is difficult to imagine how the four officers intended to carry out these threats; did they believe the eighteen powerful men would simply bend over a convenient rock to be whipped? Stand by at attention, saluting the Union Jack perhaps while their leaders were being executed by firing squad? Slavery was, of course, still a standard in the 1820 "civilized" world but Canadian voyageurs were free men, extremely proud of their skills and hired by the job or the season. Fortunately for Franklin, before any punishments had to be attempted "four [Indian] hunters arrived, bringing the flesh of two reindeer [i.e., caribou], and after this period we suffered no more from deficiency of provisions, nor were we [i.e., the officers] again censured for temerity: the Canadians never exercising reflection unless they are hungry." Such a remark from Hood, the gentlest of the officers, pinpoints the English attitude early in the expedition. The voya-

23

geurs have literally carried them over two thousand miles into the country, nevertheless they are little more than thoughtless hirelings of burden who, despite their acknowledged excessive burdens, must be kept in place by threat and physical punishment.

By August 20 the torturously moving expedition finally reaches Winter Lake where on the edge of the treeline they intend to build Fort Enterprise and winter over. Hood records that the expedition had moved 1516 miles in the brief summer of 1820 but is still over 300 miles from the Arctic coast. But they are full of hope. It is fortunate for them that the Indian hunters can supply them with plenty of meat (Winter Lake to this day is within the wintering area for the Beverly herd of caribou) so that for some months the Canadians do not again need to "exercise reflection."

By October 9 the river is filming with ice, though the lake has been firmly frozen for two weeks. The three buildings of "Fort" Enterprise have been built of logs in the French Canadian post-and-lintel style, the largest being separate quarters and mess for the four officers. They enter again the arctic winter stillness. Within a year young Hood, the most gifted and promising of the officers, will have entered his ultimate stillness. He will not die of overwork and starvation, though he will be on the extremest edge of exactly that. A year later on October 7, 1821, Richardson and Hepburn will be left alone with Hood on the tundra somewhere between the Obstruction Rapids on the Coppermine River and Fort Enterprise; Back and Franklin and those few voyageurs still alive will be struggling ahead through the snow to try to find the Yellowknife Indians who alone can save them all from death by starvation. They have stayed too long on the coast, mapping its complexities and so have fallen behind the fall migration of the caribou southward. There is literally nothing on the tundra to hunt. They have eaten their last bit of caribou on September 14; since then they have tried to subsist somehow on the occasional ptarmigan and boiled moss, *tripe de roche* as they dignify it with French, though to be completely frank, it makes them shit more than they eat. They have laboured over 1224 miles of rivers and coast that summer, the last 300 miles on foot with the voyageurs sinking in September snow under ninety-pound packs because the freezing rivers and rapids have finished what the sea had begun in destroying their canoes. Hood, who has always walked second in breaking trail because he makes the compass readings that keep them on their correct linear route while the leading trailbreakers spell each other off, Hood can walk no further. On October 7, 1821, Richardson records:

After Captain Franklin had bidden us farewell we [i.e., Hood, Richardson and Hepburn] remained seated by the fireside as long as the willows the men had cut for us before they departed, lasted. We had no *tripe de roche* that day, but drank an infusion of the country tea-plant [Labrador tea?], which was grateful from its warmth, although it afforded no sustenance. We then retired to bed, where we remained all the next day, as the weather was stormy, and the snow-drift so heavy as to destroy every prospect of success in our endeavours to light a fire with the green and frozen willows, which were our only fuel. Through the extreme kindness and forethought of a lady, the party, previous to leaving London, had been furnished with a small collection of religious books, of which we still retained two or three of the most portable, and they proved of incalculable benefit to us. We read portions of them to each other as we lay in bed, in addition to the morning and evening service, and found that they inspired us on each perusal with so strong a sense of the omnipresence of a beneficent God, that our situation, even in these wilds, appeared no longer destitute; and we conversed, not only with calmness, but with cheerfulness, detailing with unrestrained confidence the past events of our lives, and dwelling with hope on our future prospects. Had my poor friend been spared to

25

revisit his native land, I should look back to this period with unalloyed delight.

One of their books is of course the *Book of Common Prayer* whose lectionary gives them their daily morning and evening readings. The reading for October 7 is II Corinthians 6; perhaps the following passage was especially encouraging to Hood:

We then, as workers together with him, beseech you also that ye receive not the grace of God in vain. . . .
But in all things approving ourselves as the ministers of God, in much patience, in afflictions, in necessities, in distresses,
In stripes, in imprisonments, in tumults, in labours, in watchings, in fastings;
By pureness, by knowledge, by longsuffering, by kindness, by the Holy Ghost, by love unfeigned. . . .
By honour and dishonour, by evil report and good report: as deceivers, and yet true;
As unknown, and yet well known; as dying and, behold, we live. . . .

Or the reading for October 8:

Having therefore these promises, dearly beloved, let us cleanse ourselves from all filthiness of the flesh and spirit, perfecting holiness in the fear of God . . . For godly sorrow [and suffering] worketh repentance to salvation not to be repented of: but the sorrow of the world worketh death.

Or for October 9:

For ye know the grace of our Lord Jesus Christ, that, though he was rich, yet for your sakes he became poor, that ye through his poverty might be rich.

One might well ask what is faith for if it cannot guide us, as here, in considering our mortality. Two years later when John Richardson is safely back in England, he writes Hood's father:

It was during our perilous march across the Barren Grounds that we unbosomed ourselves to each other, and our conversation tended to excite in us mutually a firm reliance on the wisdom and beneficence of the decrees of the Almighty. Our sufferings were never acute during the march, the sensation of hunger ceased after the third day of privation, and with the decay of strength, the love of life also decayed. We could calmly contemplate the approach of death, and our feelings were excited only by the idea of the grief of our relatives.

Besides the Bible, they read Edward Bickersteth's *A Scripture Help*, and a prayer of the Princess Elizabeth of France, "which, amongst others, had been presented by a lady before the expedition left England," is repeated often by Hood in his last days:

What may befall me this day, O God, I know not. But I know that nothing can happen to me which Thou hast not foreseen, ruled, willed, and ordained from all eternity, and that suffices me. I adore Thy eternal and inscrutable designs. I submit to them with all my heart through love to Thee. I accept all, I make unto Thee a sacrifice of all, and to this poor sacrifice I add that of my Divine Saviour. In His name, and for the sake of His infinite merits, I ask of Thee that I may be endowed with patience under suffering and with the perfect submission which is due to all which Thou willest or permittest.

Hood can no longer move; he can barely lift his head. All three are freezing to death, starving, motionless spots in a tiny clump of willows in a hollow of the tundra. They still feel "the omnipresence of a beneficent God" in their overwhelming stillness.

On October 9 a critical event takes place. Michel Terohaute, the Iroquois voyageur, returns to them from Franklin who is still struggling to get to Fort Enterprise and the hoped-for help from Akaitcho and the Yellowknife people. Michel brings a rabbit and a ptarmigan but, as Richardson writes, he

complained of cold, and Mr. Hood offered to share his buffalo robe with him at night; I gave him one of the two shirts which I wore, whilst Hepburn, in the warmth of his heart, exclaimed, "How I shall love this man if I find he does not tell lies like the others." . . . after reading the evening service we retired to bed full of hope.

The arctic experience has drastically altered their class behavior: they now share clothes and blankets. Next day Michel, oddly, asks for a hatchet to go hunting; a hunter invariably uses only a gun and a knife. He returns with what he says is the frozen meat of a wolf gored by a caribou; they eat the meat chopped from the carcass, but Richardson becomes convinced that it may be part of the body of one of Franklin's voyageurs frozen farther ahead on the trail to Fort Enterprise. However they dare say nothing since Michel, besides his strange moodiness, is armed and obviously much stronger than they three together. Motionless they wait for help to come, growing steadily weaker. On Sunday, October 20, after the morning service Hepburn is trying to cut willows and Richardson scraping *tripe de roche* off some rocks when they hear Michel quarreling with Hood. A shot goes off. Richardson hurries up fearing Hood in despair has killed himself. His poor friend is most certainly dead, the Bible still in his hand. The morning reading for October 20 is Leviticus 9 and 10:

And it came to pass on the eighth day [in the wilderness of Sinai] that Moses called Aaron and his sons, and the elders of Israel;

And he said unto Aaron, Take thee a young calf for a sin offering, and a ram for a burnt offering, without blemish, and offer them before the Lord.

And unto the children of Israel thou shalt speak, saying, Take ye a kid of the goats for a sin offering; . . .

Also a bullock and a ram for peace offerings, to sacrifice before the Lord; and a meat offering mingled with oil: for today the Lord will appear unto you.

For Hood, in wilderness and sacrifice the Lord has truly appeared.

28

Richardson had expected Hood's death for days; he himself is barely alive, yet when he examines his friend closely he realizes he has been shot in the back of the head: "the muzzle of the [long rifle] had been applied so close as to set fire to the nightcap behind." Michel, watching the doctor and holding another rifle, insists he knows nothing; Hood's gun just went off, he says. What can the Englishmen do?

We removed the body into a clump of willows behind the tent, and, returning to the fire, read the funeral service in addition to evening prayers.

That they seem to have mourned all day he does not mention. They must now try to reach Fort Enterprise on their own: the rescue party Franklin promised to send back has not come. Unencumbered by the dying Hood, and cooking pieces of his scraped buffalo robe for food, they set out. Michel always keeps himself armed and between the other two. Finally on the trail on October 23 (fifteen days after Franklin left them behind) the ever-watchful voyageur drops back a little and Richardson reports:

Hepburn and I were now left together for the first time since Mr. Hood's death, and he acquainted me with several material circumstances which he had observed of Michel's behaviour, and which confirmed me in the opinion that there was no safety for us except in his death, and he [Hepburn] offered to be the instrument of it. I determined, however, as I was thoroughly convinced of the necessity of such a dreadful act, to take the whole responsibility upon myself; and immediately upon Michel's coming up, I put an end to his life by shooting him through the head with a pistol. Had my own life alone been threatened, I would not have purchased it by such a measure; but I considered myself as intrusted also with the protection of Hepburn's, a man, who, by his humane attentions and devotedness, had so endeared himself to me, that I felt more anxiety for his safety than for my own.

At this point of "execution," as Richardson and Franklin both called it (did Richardson in pulling the trigger recall his

captain's threat of "the heaviest punishment" against the voyageur complainers?), a review of the expedition's achieve-
ment and method will explain what the arctic landscape had
perforce done to the usual English standards of conduct.
Supported by Indian hunters they had left Fort Enterprise on
June 4, 1821, and paddled down the Coppermine River
north; by July 19 they at last reached the open ocean. There
the Indians left them and a support party of five whites
returned overland. Though this party suffered much hard-
ship (going eleven days without meat), all five survived the
trail back to the trading post on Great Slave Lake. Mean-
while, facing the ocean encumbered with cakes of ice,
Richardson writes that the remaining eleven voyageurs
"seem terrified at the idea of a voyage through an icy sea in
bark canoes" and indeed one might ask, why should they not
be? They had only two fragile canoes, one of which a week
later was very nearly crushed between two ice floes. There
was not a birch tree for repair, nor any tree for that matter,
within hundreds of miles. Nevertheless they did travel;
incredibly. By the end of August, after coasting along the
Arctic shore for almost six hundred miles, traversing bays of
open ocean whose headlands they could not see, the birchbark is almost falling from the gunwales and Richardson
still, amazingly, records:

The fears of our voyageurs have now entirely mastered their prudence and they are not restrained by the presence of their officers
from giving loose to a free and sufficiently rude expression of their
feelings.

"Mastered their prudence" indeed! One assumes that Franklin, had he been on board ship, would have keel-hauled
them in the face of what they recognized as their imminent
death: "They despair of ever seeing home again . . . [they say]
any attempt to proceed further [is] little short of madness."

The voyageurs are, of course, deadly right. They know they have been too long on the sea and that the annual caribou migration has left them behind. With the wood and bark of one ruined canoe they cook their last full meal of muskox meat on September 4. The other canoe is destroyed while crossing the Burnside River on September 8. The officers, good seamen all, know the compass course to reach Fort Enterprise and they begin to walk through the sudden and terrifyingly early snow and cold across the tundra. Each voyageur carries a ninety-pound pack; not one of them has any idea what lies in their path and they can eat only what they can find to hunt, daily: if there were some food to carry it would simply increase their enormous burden.

In their path are three unknown and unfordable rivers; they are slivered with ice, but of course the men cannot wait for them to freeze because they have no food. They manage to cross the Cracroft and Burnside rivers without any fatal accidents, though disaster is barely averted at the Belanger Rapids. The Coppermine River rushing over the double Obstruction Rapids really destroys them. They are stopped there for eleven days, wearing away their last reserves of strength in a desperate search for a means to cross. Finally Pierre St. Germain manages to build a tiny shell out of willows and the oilcloth with which the officers cover their sleeping robes and hauls them all across the vicious river one at a time on a line he strings. By then one of their men, the Inuit translator Junius, has disappeared somewhere never to be seen again. They are less than sixty miles from Fort Enterprise and Franklin sends George Back ahead fast with three of the strongest voyageurs to try to contact the Yellowknife Indians. The main party trudges on as slowly as the weakest man can move; gradually the men, so long overworked while subsisting mostly on boiled leather and moss, when they can find it, begin to fall behind.

Now Franklin and his party are forced to make certain decisions: everyone is so weak they can barely walk by themselves — they certainly cannot carry the dying. So they do exactly what the Inuit were traditionally forced to do under those circumstances. Tony Thrasher in his book *Thrasher . . . Skid Row Eskimo* explains such behavior, behavior which Canadians to this day consider only in terms of "savagery." Thrasher records that in 1960 at Spence Bay:

> I met a boy there who had experienced some hardships in life. One winter, his grandfather, mother, and three little brothers and sisters got caught in a big storm on a journey and were starving to death. The old man called to his grandson. He told him, "I am no more good and I am just a burden, a load for you, so if you want to live, kill me so I'll stop suffering and it will be easier for the rest of you." The old man made him put a gun to his head and pull the trigger. The young boy . . . nine or ten years old then . . . did it as a favour to his grandfather. After the old man died, the mother, to lighten their load, dug a hole in the snow and put caribou skins in it. Then she put her two little ones in the hole, covered them up to keep them warm, and journeyed off into the storm for home with her boy and baby. Sometime afterwards, she returned to the place with her boy to retrieve the two children, but they had frozen to death.

Franklin faces exactly that situation since his voyageurs, even without a much-reduced pack, can no longer carry their bodies across the endless tundra. But he does not of course shoot those men too weak to keep up, though that might have been a final desperate act of kindness. No. He leaves them behind. Here is a roll call of those men who, on a quest whose purpose none of them could fathom, nevertheless made possible the journey and all the honours Franklin and Richardson and Back were to receive later:

Junius: Eskimo translator, canoeman; vanished September 27, 1821, without crossing the Coppermine River.

Mathew Pelonquin: voyageur, unable to keep up, left behind after Obstruction Rapids on October 6.

Registe Vaillant: voyageur, collapsed, left behind some hours later on October 6.

Jean Baptiste Belanger: voyageur, collapsed, left behind October 7.

Ignace Perrault: voyageur, collapsed, left behind October 8.

Antonio Fontano: Italian voyageur, collapsed, left behind October 8. Franklin promised him that, if he survived, he would assist him to return to Italy to see his dying father.

Gabriel Beauparlant: voyageur, collapsed at Round Rock Lake while looking for Indians with Back's party, left behind October 16.

Michel Terohaute: Iroquois voyageur, shot by Richardson on October 23; he lived on either Belanger's or Perrault's frozen flesh and undoubtedly fed some of it to Hood, Richardson and Hepburn.

Joseph Peltier: voyageur, died of malnutrition after the Franklin party reached Fort Enterprise, November 1.

Francois Samandre: voyageur, died of malnutrition at Fort Enterprise, November 2.

Only *Pierre St. Germain*, a Metis and Yellowknife Indian interpreter, the best hunter of all whose skill in somehow fashioning a shell out of oilskins saved the party at the Coppermine River, and the two strongest voyageurs, *Solomon Belanger* and *Joseph Benoit*, survived that dreadful trek.

Four of the five Englishmen, however, survived. It cannot be because they were physically stronger than the Canadians. Whatever food there was was always divided by

Hood as long as he lived with scrupulous honesty (he invariably took, writes Franklin, the smallest share for himself), so this pattern of deaths must have come about because the Canadians laboured more, carrying the heavier loads. It would seem that the English officers survive on the Arctic tundra because (a) they leave behind their dying (though they sincerely promise to return with help if they can find it), (b) they eat human flesh (though inadvertently, and horrified at the very thought), and (c) they kill the strongest man in the party because they are afraid he will kill and probably eat them. Later Willard Wentzel, the Northwest Company clerk in charge at Fort Providence, accuses Dr. Richardson of murder, but no investigation is ever made beyond Richardson's report. Yet a hundred years later when two Inuit hunters kill two priests on the lower Coppermine River because they are afraid the priests with their rifles would kill them, those two Inuit men are taken through three years of Canadian judicial systems and courts to be declared guilty of murder. A special law for whites persists in the North.

Lieutenant George Back confesses to Wentzel the next summer (1822) that "to tell the truth, Wentzel, things have taken place which must not be told." What were these untellable secrets? Richardson presumably tells some of his: he shot and killed Michel Terohaute; he privately writes about perhaps, unknowingly, eating human flesh. Franklin vanishes in 1845 telling nothing of any "secrets." Back himself leads several important Arctic expeditions and dies knighted, an admiral, fifty-seven years later without ever saying anything.

There was one other Englishman there: ordinary seaman John Hepburn who on October 28, 1821, more or less carries Dr. Richardson, who is on the verge of death by mal-nutrition, into an empty, cold Fort Enterprise where a starv-ing Franklin and four other men greet them with "melan-choly satisfaction." There are no Indian hunters near Fort Enterprise; there is no food. They burn the fort log by log to keep warm; on last year's garbage heap they find half-rotted caribou hides which they eat boiled. The warblefly larvae imbedded in the hides are especially nutritious: indeed, those tiny bits of protein undoubtedly prolong the lives of the three Englishmen and two voyageurs until the Yellow-knife Indians arrive with meat on November 7. But thirty years later "excellent old Mr. Hepburn," then serving on board the *Prince Albert* which is searching for the lost Frank-lin expedition, tells Captain Kennedy and Joseph René Bel-lot, who records it, that during the first winter in Fort Enter-prise, 1820,

[Hood] and [Back] had a quarrel about an Indian woman, and were to fight a duel; but he [i.e., Hepburn] overheard them and drew the charges of the pistols at night.

On October 18, 1820, Franklin sent Back on a five-month trip to return to Fort Chipewyan for supplies and thus left the field of romance, it would seem, to Hood. The woman they quarreled about was the daughter of an old Yellow-knife guide named Keskarrah whose ulcerated wife was being cared for by Dr. Richardson. Notes Franklin in his 1823 *Narrative*:

The daughter, whom we designated Green-stockings from her dress, is considered by her tribe to be a great beauty. Mr. Hood drew an accurate portrait of her, although her mother was averse to her sitting for it. She was afraid, she said, that her daughter's like-ness would induce the great Chief who resided in England to send for the original. The young lady, however, was undeterred by any such fear. She has already been an object of contest between her countrymen, and although under sixteen years of age, has belonged

35

successively to two husbands, and would probably have been the wife of many more, if her mother had not required her services as a nurse.

Franklin no doubt drew an English chuckle about the mother's naive fears regarding royal customs, but I'm certain those fears were based on white behavior the Indian women knew only too well. His euphemism of "husband" clearly reveals his opinion of Green Stockings' morality; but he says nothing about his young officers' considering Green Stockings a great beauty also, to the point of being prepared to kill each other over her. The only other expedition detail on Green Stockings is given by Richardson who notes the next summer (July 8, 1821): "Broadface, one of our (Yellowknife) hunters being enamoured of [Keskarrah's] daughter, chose to stay on the Coppermine River...."

Perhaps Broadface is one of the numerous "husbands" Franklin mentions; he rarely records the name of an Indian. Back's portrait of a Broad Face, painted during the second expedition at Fort Franklin six years after Hood's death, shows a cute, almost baby-faced Indian whose almond eyes and pouted lips could as easily be female as male. But one would expect that Hood's portrait of Green Stockings, apparently the only woman he painted in Canada, should reveal some hint of his feeling. In the coloured engraving which Franklin includes in his *Narrative* (the original is lost) Green Stockings is seated at the feet of her father who stands, arms folded inside his blanket, in profile on the right. She is full face, sits with her legs folded left, a narrow Yellowknife snowshoe which she is mending in her lap. She wears heavy furs and green cloth leggings ending in moccasins; her face is framed by thick hair cropped shaggy, shoulder length; her eyes look up from under heavy brows, peering intently; her face is still and regular, it could easily be masculine. Hood was an excellent portrait painter, as his picture of the chief Akaitcho and his son proves. When he painted Green Stockings could he not allow himself any ease, any relaxation of the beauty his picture called for? Why, during that interminable winter in Fort Enterprise when he had months to fashion the one woman whom, as far as we can know, he loved in his brief life, when he deliberately drew her in the snowshoe image of the Yellowknife creation myth, why was his eye so dark, his hand so stiff?

Perhaps when he painted her he already knew that Green Stockings was carrying his child, and what hope could he have for such an infant? Perhaps he had already been forced by Franklin, in the name of English Christian morality and the expedition, to leave her for the next Indian "husband" who could forcibly take her. The fact is that nowhere, ever, does Hood mention her in his diary. Nor does Richardson in his 1822 letter to Hood's father. In 1851 good old Mr. Hepburn tells Bellot confidentially at one of their long story-telling sessions aboard the *Prince Albert*, one of the many ships sent out to look for a Franklin finally lost and even in August already stuck in the ice: "Poor [Hood] had by the same woman a daughter, whom his family have recently sent for."

He makes it sound as if a servant is finally being sent to fetch someone from across the street. Did that daughter ever travel to England? After thirty years without any recognized English existence, who decided to "send for" her? Why? Did she accept the sending for? Was she still alive? No one knows. C. Stuart Houston quotes Clifford Wilson, editor of *The Beaver*, as writing in 1953 that the 1823 census at Fort Resolution listed a child as "the orphaned daughter of Lieutenant Hood." No corroborating evidence has yet been found, but it would seem the good Yellowknife people of the North did not hesitate to speak of Hood's secret, though the English did. And how reliable is Hepburn's "downstairs" gossip? There is no record to indicate that the Reverend Dr. Richard Hood of Bury, Lancashire, ever heard of the only child his "dear, dear Robert, the pride of my little family, to whom I looked as a chief source of consolation in my declining years," left for his possible "consolation."

In 1821 there were only some two hundred Yellowknife Indians in existence; they hunted around the northern and eastern shores of Great Slave Lake up to Great Bear Lake and the treeline. When their chief Akaitcho sees the expedition off for the Arctic Ocean in June 1821, he says he has "not the least hopes of ever seeing one person return." However, when the Yellowknives hear of the expedition's distress on November 3, 1821, they immediately dispatch three hunters with some of their own scarce meat to rescue the white men left dying at Fort Enterprise. These laden hunters walk fifty-five miles in two-and-a-half days and save their lives. The Indians, Richardson writes to his wife, "wept on beholding the deplorable condition to which we were reduced." Another party arrives a few days later with more supplies and clothing. By November 16 all are strong enough to start for the Indian camps. On the journey:

The Indians treated us with the utmost tenderness, gave us their snow-shoes ... keeping by our sides, that they might lift us when we fell. ... The Indians ... cooked for us, and fed us as if we had been children; evincing a degree of humanity that would have done honour to the most civilized nation.

Finally on November 25 they approach the first camp, which contains the parents of Akaitcho's wife:

These good old people welcomed us with the utmost kindness and entreated us to remain with them for the night which we did, whilst

Thoveeyorre went on to the leader who was in an encampment further off. The old woman shewed her stock of meat and desired us to take what we liked best, but after witnessing Hepburn's awkward attempt at cookery arising from his weakness, she herself culled out the most delicate bits and cooking them expressed much satisfaction in seeing us eat. Many others of the Indians, also came to see us in the afternoon, and most of them presented us with meat, so that we were surrounded with more than we could consume in a week.

At the chief's camp Franklin is mortified to find that the supplies he expected from England have not arrived at Fort Providence with the fur packet that summer. Because the fur traders too are low on supplies, and he has had problems with them regarding his admiralty requisitions anyway, Franklin has literally nothing with which to repay the Yellowknives who have saved their lives. He can only give them promises, as he has in the past. However here again Akaitcho proves his human dignity:

Akaitcho with his whole band came to the Fort [Providence] in the afternoon. He smoked his customary pipe, with M^r. Weekes in the hall, and learnt from him that our expected supplies had not come in. Afterwards in a conference with Captain Franklin he spoke of this circumstance as a disappointment indeed, sufficiently severe to himself, to whom his band looked up for the support of their interests, but without attaching any blame to us. "The world goes badly" he said, "all are poor. You are poor, the traders appear to be poor, I and my party are poor likewise, and since the goods have not come in we cannot have them. I do not regret having supplied you with provisions, for a Red Knife [i.e. Yellowknife] can never permit a White man to suffer from want on his lands, without flying to his aid. I trust however that we shall, as you say, receive what is due to us, next autumn, and at all events," he added in a tone of good humour, "it is the first time that the White people have been indebted to the Red Knife People."

A mere three years later these kind, gracious people had almost disappeared. They had warred so incessantly with their traditional enemies the Dogribs that by 1824 they were almost annihilated. In 1833 George Back is in command of his own canoe expedition and encounters Akaitcho and his few followers again, now themselves starving in the poor hunting country to which they have been driven east of Great Slave Lake. But the moral grandeur of the chief remains. "Alas!" he says to Back, "how many [of my people] sleep with our fathers! But the Great Chief trusts us; and it is better that ten Indians should perish, than that one white man should suffer through our negligence." After all, he explains, Indians are accustomed to starving but Whites are not.

And then, on July 3, 1834, Back again meets:

my old acquaintance and Indian belle ... Green Stockings. Though surrounded by a family, with one urchin in her cloak clinging to her back, and sundry other maternal accompaniments, I immediately recognised her, and called her by her name; at which she laughed, and said "she was an old woman now," [she is thirty] — begging, at the same time, that she might be relieved by the "medicine man [i.e. Richard King], for she was very much out of health." However, notwithstanding all this, she was still the beauty of her tribe; and, with that consciousness which belongs to all belles, savage or polite, seemed by no means displeased when I sketched her portrait.

Back seems very cool about his old flame, as he must in his official report, but his second in command, Dr. Richard King, deliberately reminds the reader of Hood in his published description of the encounter. He writes, almost contradicting Back:

It was not a little singular that I should have been the first to recognise Green-stocking; but, since my return to England, having compared the engraving of her from a drawing by the late Lieutenant Hood with my recollection of her countenance, I am not surprised at the circumstance. It must have been at the time it was taken a very faithful representation; for although much older and careworn, the resemblance appeared to me exceedingly striking.

40

Notwithstanding her state of ill health and inferiority to the other females of the tribe in exterior embellishments, (her increasing family having reduced her to abject poverty,) she still remained by far the prettiest woman among them.

Did King, who was critical of Back's expedition leadership, take this dig at his commander's eye and portrait skills? He alone records that in 1834 Back was using a camera lucida to draw portraits, an instrument of mirrors where rays of light throw an exact image on paper so it can be easily traced. Back's 1834 portrait has never been found. All that is clear is that Green Stockings had survived the Indian wars. Was one of her "increasing family" Hood's "orphaned" fourteen-year-old daughter? Perhaps she was a beauty also and already "married" as her mother had been twice at sixteen? Back admits nothing of his personal feelings or knowledge. Did mother and daughter survive until 1851 when Hepburn tells his story? Green Stockings would then have been forty-six years old, a most venerable age. Who can know? One thing is certain, tiny Greenstocking Lake and the huge Hood River, which plunges over Wilberforce Falls into the Arctic on Bathurst Inlet, lie on opposite sides of the continental divide. They have no connection with each other, except perhaps somewhere in the Arctic Ocean.

Today in half a day's travel from my home I am flying over the astonishing, immense delta of the Mackenzie River, which Alexander Mackenzie reached in only two weeks by canoe from Great Slave Lake in 1789; which Franklin and Back and Richardson (without Hood of course) on their second expedition reach in six months from London (via New York and the Methye portage) in light wooden boats of their own design, August 16, 1825. They build and winter in Fort Franklin on Great Bear Lake and in the summer of 1826 Richardson leads one part of the expedition east exploring all the Arctic coast between the mouth of the Mackenzie and the mouth of the Coppermine. In the meantime Back and Franklin explore west, intending to rendezvous with Captain Frederick Beechey who is sailing the *Blossom* around South America and up the length of the Pacific through the Bering Strait. But Franklin never meets Beechey; two years later the captains discover they were within one hundred and forty miles of each other along what is today the north coast of Alaska; unfortunately at that time these one hundred and forty miles were hidden by solid pack ice and impenetrable fog, that is, by water in its more arctic forms. Franklin the sailor was again beset by the problem of a linear movement becoming an areal stillness he did not know how to deal with.

Literary critic Ian MacLaren has pointed out the irony of the expedition's immobilization on that coast, an ironic foreshadowing of what would happen in a more massive and terrifying way in 1846 on the shore of King William Island where, unknown to himself freezing in his inert frozen ships, Franklin will actually have discovered the best navigable Northwest Passage (there are really four unnavigable passages through the archipelago). MacLaren summarizes Franklin's dilemma in 1826 facing a stillness enforced upon him by the particular landscape he is giving his life to explore:

Inland "excursions" or "rambles" were precluded both by the "mosquitoes, which were so numerous as to prevent any enjoyment of the open air, and to keep us confined to a tent filled with smoke," and by the terrain itself: "even had the mosquitoes been less than tormenting, the swampiness of the ground, in which we sank ancle-deep at every step, deprived us of the pleasure of walking." "There was," Franklin despairs, "literally nothing to do." Thus, a supreme incongruity manifests itself: a man who defined himself, indeed understood himself, in terms of his explorations [i.e. motion] had nothing to explore [i.e. cannot move].

But when one personally goes to the Mackenzie Delta, Franklin and Richardson seem amazingly irrelevant. There they appear little more than the typical wilfully blind or at best only partially seeing men who will force themselves upon a landscape, will try to bulldoze their way through whatever confronts them and who, when this deliberate blindness kills their companions and, eventually, themselves, will become heroes to be forever memorialized. If I were deeply cynical I might point out that the historical record implies that the greater the numbers of their fellow heroes they take with them in death, the greater the so-called heroism and of course the proportionately larger the resulting memorials.

However, on a tributary of the Mackenzie River, the Peel, such thoughts seem to me unimportant; at best merely clever. The Peel River rises in the Ogilvie and Wernecke mountains of the Yukon, flows eastward through the giant canyons it forms between the Mackenzie Mountains to the south and the Richardson Mountains to the north, then it bends sharply left, that is, north to parallel the Mackenzie until it becomes in effect the West or Husky Channel of the giant delta. Among the upthrust crags of the Ogilvies and the Werneckes, the sources of the Peel — the Snake, the Bonnet Plume, the Wind, the Hart, the Blackstone, the Ogilvie rivers — are clear, transparent braids of water twisting their diaphanous patterns over gravel, between rocks; but at Fort McPherson the Peel River is brown and thick as mud, totally impenetrable. Your hand vanishes when you touch it; it could be bearing a hundred submerged bodies past you and you would know nothing. Like the Mackenzie River after it is joined by the relentless Liard River, the Peel is strange and secret. It reveals nothing at all; only glistening surface.

Three ravens on a crossing of driftwood logs tossed up on the muddy river's edge observe me. Occasionally one squawks, lowering and stretching and bobbing its neck in that particular ravenesque way which appears so oddly investigative, almost voyeuristic. I remember that according to a Mackenzie Inuit story the raven has little to thank man for. In 1913 a woman named Unilina told it this way:

It is said that long ago the raven and the loon met and began talking. They agreed to make each other look beautiful, and the raven began with the loon. He marked him all over with black dots, drew lines on his body and painted his bill yellow. When he finished, the loon began on the raven by painting him basic black all over. But, before he could do anything else, a man came along and frightened them both away. The raven was never finished, and has remained black to this day.

I want to reassure these awesome birds that I had nothing to do with their black fate, but I doubt if they would believe a man, especially a white one, anything. Farther north among willows is a Loucheux summer fish camp; a canoe with two tiny bumps of people bobbing towards nets hovers there on the distant surface where the river seems to bend. Though I cannot see it from here, I know the floats holding those nets will be plastic cooking oil jugs, or stove fuel tins from Esso. I am eating Brunswick Canadian Sardines, product of Connors Bros. Ltd., Black's Harbour, New Brunswick. One and then another of the ravens tires of my motionlessness and lifts itself away, easily, into the air. Above the bristle of spruce on the layered river banks opposite me is the distant grey outline of the Richardson Mountains. In July 1931, Albert Johnson floated by here on a three-log raft to build his fateful cabin up the Rat River in the foothills of those mountains. Secrets; secrets everywhere.

The last raven is watching me intensely. Perhaps it

intends to tell me that this is not the same river that Johnson journeyed on. It never is. But the single raven does not move and it makes no sound; after all, everyone knows that three may keep a secret if two of them are dead. Not necessarily, but they *may*. The only motion or sound is that of the river, and I do not understand that. The motionless silence of the raven tells me that the secret will have to be transformed into mystery before I can understand; know.

II

ON BEING MOTIONLESS

Singing was just an ordinary hunting
method. The Inuit used to make up
lots of songs — all kinds of different songs
to make it easier to hunt the animals. They sang
to get the animals used to the hunters.
Those early people were very clever.
We now have guns; in the old days
people just used their voices.

Peter Pitseolak, *People From Our Side*, 1975

The Inuit understanding of visible phenomena is expressed by their language as two dimensional: the very grammar of Inuktitut requires that you express all phenomena as either roughly equal in size — things are as broad as they are long, that is, *areal*, or as unequal — they are longer than they are broad, that is, *linear*. This understanding explains why it is really impossible for a living being to be ultimately lost on the vast expanses of the arctic landscape, either tundra or ice.

Two corollaries expand this linguistic structural under-standing and further explain what I mean: first, an areal thing changes dimension and becomes linear when it moves; second, any area without easily observable limits (a field of ice, the sea, an expanse of tundra) is automatically classified as long and narrow, that is, as linear also. In order to live a human being must move; to live in the Arctic a human being must, generally speaking, move quite a lot to acquire enough food. Therefore in order to live he/she must become a linear dimension in a linear space. That means that another moving person (also linear) will certainly find them because even in the largest space their moving lines must at some point intersect, and the very rarity of those lines in the "empty" Arctic makes them all the more conspicuous.

All this changes radically of course when the human being's dimension changes back to areal, that is, the person becomes motionless. To locate a body may take very long; to find even a few of Franklin's 130 dead sailors took thirteen years, and Andrée, the Swedish lighter-than-air balloonist and his two assistants who began their misconceived drift for the North Pole on July 11, 1897, were not found until July 9, 1930, and that by accident. A body may truly be lost forever, even if it quickly freezes and lasts for years. But on the so-called empty barrens of the Arctic it is actually impossible for a living person to stay lost; or by the same token, it is impossible to hide.

Aklavik (an Inuktitut word which means the "Place of the Brown Bear") is today a cluster of seven hundred and fifty people almost invisible in the enormous Mackenzie Delta. All Saints (Anglican) Church Cemetery there contains the grave of a man who tried to hide in the Arctic. Albert Johnson, as he is called, should have known better. He never saw Aklavik alive; he was brought there only to be buried and since he had killed one policeman and almost killed two others he was buried on March 9, 1932, as far away from the tiny log church as possible, on the edge of church property in unhallowed ground, as they say. However, since 1932 the town has grown; the brown log church has become a museum and a new prefab structure stands there bluer than the sky. The town is today so large that Main Street with its two stores, hamlet offices and fire station runs along the back of the cemetery. As a result Albert Johnson's grave now borders on Main Street: the entrance to the cemetery is right there beside two broken tree stumps, trees once planted on the grave itself and now dead, that stick like symbolic rotten columns out of the picket fence outlining his gravesite. One stump has a large white *A* painted on it, the other an even larger *J*. Beside the grave stands a square sign with crudely painted scenes from Johnson's life. It bears the following legend:

THE MADTRAPPER
ALBERT JOHNSON
ARRIVED IN ROSS
RIVER AUG. 21, 1927
COMPLAINTS OF
LOCAL TRAPPERS
BROUGHT THE RCMP
ON HIM HE SHOT TWO
OFFICERS AND BE-
CAME A FUGITIVE OF
THE LAW WITH HOWL-
ING HUSKIES, DANGER
OUS TRAILS, FROZEN
NIGHTS. THE POSSE
FINALLY CAUGHT UP
WITH HIM. HE WAS
KILLED UP THE
EAGLE RIVER
FEB 17, 1932

The slender white crosses, the picket fences of the graves of the good Aklavik citizens crowd about, spreading to the distant corners of the large graveyard, but only this once ostracized "fugitive of the law" who according to the sign was apparently hunted for four-and-a-half years receives so much attention. Every tourist goes there to take a picture. Why are murderers so much remembered?

I should talk! I've written a story, several articles, a movie script, a novel about that man and now he has returned to haunt these essays! I will not tell his well-known story here; at the moment I wish to use him as the most obvious example of a person in the North with a secret, and in contemplating Albert Johnson's secret I believe some of the wider secrets of the arctic landscape will become clearer. At least I trust their outlines will.

In one of the most beautiful short stories ever written, "The Lady with the Pet Dog," Anton Chekhov has his protagonist recognize:

The personal life of every individual is based on secrecy, and perhaps it is for that reason that civilized people insist so strongly that personal privacy be respected.

Chekhov's protagonist, Gurov, is thinking of the double life he personally leads. Gurov recognizes that "he had two lives, an open one," which is the conventional public one that everyone knows, "and another life that went on in secret ... that no living soul knew of.... Everything of importance ... everything about which [he] ... did not deceive himself" is in that second, secret, life.

Now despite a massive manhunt and fifty-five years of sporadic search by police and private persons, we still know nothing whatever of Albert Johnson's secret life. In fact, his public life is known for certain only from July 7, 1931, when he appears south of Aklavik in Fort McPherson until he is killed "up the Eagle River" on February 17, 1932, and he becomes a motionless dot on the river ice. His most elementary secret, that of his name, still defies discovery. The legend (I use the word in both of its possible meanings) on the grave board on Aklavik's main street, which states that Johnson "arrived in Ross River Aug. 21, 1927," is fact only if we identify him with a man who in Ross River called himself Arthur Nelson. Ross River, Yukon Territory, is as the raven flies over six hundred kilometres from Fort McPherson, Northwest Territories; it is almost twice that far by mountainous river, which is how Albert Johnson arrived there. Historian Dick North of Whitehorse has identified Johnson with Nelson, but Nelson's past, his story, seemed untraceable before Ross River. However, after twenty years of "obsession" (North himself uses that word) with Johnson/Nelson, the historian is at last positive he has found the man's real name, and with it all that vast revelation of human activity and personality, of family and past and birth and place which a public name must expose, that immense factual story which every human being in the retrospect of memory has lived. Strange to say in this strange enough matter, North believes that the fugitive's name really was Johnson; only his given name was different. Instead of the relatively distinctive "Albert," North says it was, of all things, "John." John Johnson — surely one of the most ordinary, common names possible in North America.

> My name is John Johnson
> I come from Wisconsin
> I work at the lumbermill there;
> When I go down the street
> All the people I meet
> They ask what's my name
> And I say that my name is John Johnson
> I come from. . . .

If you're old enough you'll remember that round, one in which you can circle forever. This John Johnson was not however from Wisconsin. He was born in Norway and from the age of one grew up in North Dakota; he was a convicted bank robber and horse thief by age seventeen (1915) and spent several years in various United States prisons before apparently disappearing into Canada in 1923. After years of following every shred of evidence to build his case, all North lacked to make the last, indisputable identification between the two Johnsons was Albert's fingerprints. However, the prints taken from Albert Johnson after his death have disappeared from the Royal Canadian Mounted Police files.

How it has come about that one of the most famous police forces in the world has not kept the ultimate record of an unidentified criminal I will not try to explain here (that's a complicated story also). North writes, "this left only one recourse for me, and that was to dig up Albert's body . . . he was buried in permafrost and consequently his skin probably would be in good enough shape to 'lift' the prints." On April 27, 1987, the news went round the Yukon by radio and newspaper that the hamlet of Aklavik had given Dick North permission to exhume Johnson's body.

Oddly enough, on that Monday, April 27, I was in Old Crow, the most northerly settlement in the Yukon. That evening I met some twenty Loucheux people of the Old Crow community who came to talk with me about my writing and particularly what I knew about Albert Johnson. We are talking quietly, slowly comparing bits of information when the one man who has remained standing against the wall on my left suddenly asks, "Do you know who shot him first, that Albert Johnson?"

His tone is incredibly loud in the, until then, friendly room. Everyone is peering at me intently.

"I'm not sure," I say. "Do you?"

"Sure I know," he declares, "anybody here knows that, it was Johnny Moses right from here, Old Crow, he was a special constable for the police and he had permission to shoot, he was the best shot and he fired and hit him first in the foot so he couldn't run to the bank and get away, he'd have got away, they'd of never got him, that's why he was stuck there in the middle of the Eagle River. It was Johnny Moses." And then the man is shouting, "What they say is all bullshit in all them books! Bullshit! When they got him there on the Eagle River the police shot him so full of lead they couldn't lift him into the plane, ten men couldn't lift him, he was so full of lead!"

Some of the people are smiling a little. The school principal, who is my host and apologizes later for not warning me about a possible outburst from this very man, looks most uncomfortable. What this Old Crow man says is obviously impossible, but it is not ridiculous. Once, years before in Victoria, British Columbia, when I read from *The Temptations of Big Bear* the scene of the police attack in 1885 on the Big Bear's sleeping camp at Loon Lake Crossing, a Cree Indian asked me after the reading whether I knew that the North West Mounted Police had killed over three hundred of his people there and buried them so their bodies could never be found? I knew that if such had been the case the entire band would have had to be annihilated; as it was I knew of only two men actually shot and killed there while an old woman on the retreat hanged herself in terror. But it seemed to me then, and it seems to me also in Old Crow, that the story I am hearing is far from ridiculous. Something beyond mere facts is being told, a truth only words, not facts, can create. But before I have to say anything the man continues even louder:

"It was Christmas, Jesus Christ Christmas when the goddam police bang on his door, so why didn't they bring him a turkey and 'Merry Christmas' and leave him alone? Eh?"

My mind is stumbling, but I try to turn his rage a little, "Well, even if the police come banging on your house at Christmas and disturb you, you're *still* not supposed to shoot them through your door."

Some of the people chuckle with me, but for a few more moments he rants almost wildly. I am stunned; I cannot quite believe what is happening.

But it is certainly in keeping with the whole extraordinarily beautiful day. It began by flying from Dawson City, the brilliant spring sun on the snow of the Ogilvie Mountains, the sinuous bends of the Porcupine River and the tiny village set against the airstrip at the foot of Old Crow Mountain, its green spruce and streets packed in the solid snow of all-skidoo traffic. That afternoon I had given a long reading and told stories at the school and then I was taken back to the airport where the band had arranged that its plane fly me to the Richardson Mountains and the Eagle River. "We're gonna show you where Albert Johnson got shot," the pilot told me. I had never been there. With us came two Old Crow high school students who had read my novel *The Mad Trapper* and two band elders. One of them, the venerable old woman seated beside me in the Cessna, introduced herself as the sister of Johnny Moses, the RCMP special constable who had been at that shoot-out fifty-five years before, though she did not then tell me her brother had shot Albert

Johnson first. So we flew east over the widely scattered, still deserted summer fish camps and hunting camps in the snow at the caribou crossings, along the frozen river, further east until the Richardson Mountains appeared, abruptly, like enormous unglaciated pyramids folded irregularly into each other, like a random scattering of scrawled, conical shapes and all so deadly white with their creeks outlined by black spruce. Clouds covered the Barrier River Pass, which Johnson crossed in an impossible blizzard after killing Constable Edgar Millen, so we could not fly there, but the twisting loops of the Bell River, the deserted roofless walls of the three buildings of La Pierre House, the beautiful circular sweep of the Bell west around a mountain to join the Porcupine and there, just like a map, the Eagle River entering the broader Bell from the south.

We eased lower, the air as calm and solid as a rock. We saw a moose feeding among willows and the pilot laughed, "O what the hell," and went down to 150 feet and I saw tracks, mink and martin trails looping out from the river banks, even the tiny spoor of weasel, everything so icy sharp in the incredible air I had no need to breathe, only look. And then the plane made a wide turn and I saw what I had imagined, tried again and again to image years before: I saw the tight reversed S turn of the narrow river outlined by the straggling black spruce, the tight reversed S where Johnson, deceived at last by the twists of the river, ran backwards in his tracks because he thought the posse was already ahead of him and rounding the tight bend of that betrayal suddenly met the dogs, the men, the rifles racing after him head on.

It was so exactly as I had imagined it, in the plane I knew I was dreaming. It seemed I saw through that window, past the strut and the motionless wheel, under the shadow of that wing the actualization of what I had dreamt sixteen years before and then dreamt over and over again, tried to snare in the words of a short story, of a film script, of an essay, of a novel. There, on exactly such ice, between those precise tiny bristled trees; fifty-five years ago. Although of course the river under that ice could not be the same. But perhaps it was. Precisely every particle how many diurnal cycles later?

The man in the community centre at Old Crow, standing in the steady 10:30 p.m. daylight of April 27, has stopped shouting. He is talking quietly now but with very great intensity.

"Men go crazy you know," he says. "I've seen men, anybody here has seen men go really crazy. You can't help that and you should just get out of the way, leave them alone, they'll be okay, just leave them alone. Why do you have to bother a man when he goes really crazy, eh?"

Such words do not seem to expect words in reply. After a while I ask them all, "What do you think, should they dig him up now to get his fingerprints?"

Nobody says anything. "They'd probably find out for sure who he was then," I say.

A woman at the back says, "They should leave him alone."

Next morning a skidoo stops beside me as I walk down the street; it is driven by a lean, handsome man about my age in a wolverine trim parka. We met at the hall the night before and now in the sunlight he wears dark glasses so I can't see his eyes.

"I was gonna say something," he says, "but then that guy got going . . . " he shrugs.

"Oh, yeah," I say. "We talked after. He told me his father was a Danish whaler who came to Herschel Island on a whaling ship, so I asked him where were his blue eyes and blond hair."

But the skidoo driver refuses to laugh. He says instead, "Johnny Moses was my uncle. My mom lives over there, she was with you on the plane."

"Did your uncle ever talk about that manhunt?"

"Not to me."

"How come?"

He says thoughtfully, "I guess he didn't want to. He talked to my mom a lot, I know, but that's all."

"Would she talk to me about that?"

"I don't know." He is silent for a time but makes no move to go. The morning sun is almost stunning on the snow. "Once a few years before he died he was working with a construction crew near the Eagle River, they got close to that place on the river and one of the workers made a joke about it, said something like, 'Hey Johnnie, isn't this the famous place you shot Albert Johnson?' and he just put down his tools and walked away from there. Just disappeared. The foreman got worried and radioed my mom, and I went out to look for him. It took me two weeks. He was camped in the bush way up the Porcupine, just his rifle and knife. Not even a tent. He knew how to live in the bush like that."

"He came back with you?"

"Yeah. I stayed with him a few days and then we came back."

I don't know how I can ask what I want so badly to ask,

and finally I say something unnecessary; totally obvious. "He wasn't working for the police any more?"

"No. He never did after that," and it is clear from his tone what "that" is. "There was something about that Johnson . . . something strange."

That was the same word a Hareskin man from Fort Good Hope used to describe the Mackenzie River. He said it twice, very thoughtfully, remembering perhaps his lifetime beside its heavy brown darkness and all the people that had vanished into it: "The river is strange . . . strange. It will roll a body along the bottom for six days before it lifts it up so you can see it, forty miles away." That had happened to his best friend who with his girlfriend disappeared late one spring night following him in a river boat headed for Fort Good Hope. In the morning they found the boat, its kicker still idling slowly, turning circles on the river and the girl asleep huddled in the bow, still unaware that she was alone. "His body was way past Good Hope six days later, it come up. We only recognized him from the bits of clothes left on him. Sometimes they won't come up at all, if the water's too cold. Maybe in the spring, somewhere. By then you don't know them anyway."

The novel *But We Are Exiles* by Robert Kroetsch, the best novel yet written set on the Mackenzie River, opens with just such a scene. Peter Guy, pilot on the riverboat *Nahanni Jane*, is in a canoe dragging the opaque depths of the Mackenzie with grappling-hooks:

> The line in Peter's hands came taut just then; a chill shuddered up into his arms and aching neck. He heard himself yell and the skipper . . . cut off the outboard motor with a turn of a thick wrist; the canoe began to swing downstream, bow first, anchored by the quarter-inch line in Peter's hands: 'Pull him in!' the skipper shouted in the sudden silence, the motor popping and then dead.

Peter gave a jerk, another, to set the hooks, his stomach going queasy, and now the grappling-hooks and line and whatever it was they had snagged began to come up, heavy, still too far down to be seen in the sun-filtering green and then dark of the water; the line curled dripping around his high-topped boots as if to entangle him; the wet, cold line stiffened his fingers.

And bent over he could feel the stillness strike the back of his bare head, half knocking life into him, half knocking it out. His breath came in lumps. He glanced up at the breath-tripping hush; at the broad river, mirror-smooth in the afternoon sun; at the old riverboat where she lay tied up beside her two black steel barges. No one had seen the canoe stop. The lifting bow bobbed gently. He looked down again at the water and this time saw his own face watching him; the prematurely balding blond head, the full lips and squinting deep-set eyes suggesting a moodiness that didn't belong with his tall and hard body. He studied the reflection as if not sure whom he might see.

The image mimicked his hesitation, mocked his doubt by repeating it. The deep-set eyes worried against the slant of light. The mouth, pursed and offering a kiss, in its subtle retreat, threatened now to open and drown. Peter shook his head to be sure it was himself he saw. A drop of water from the rising line scarred the face, exploding its frail composure.

The grappling-hooks swam into view. They did not bring up from the darkness Michael Hornyak, burned and dead and already a little soggy — 'Goddamnit,' the skipper said. . . .

You look into the moving, dark, strange Mackenzie River and you will see nothing but yourself; though you will not appear the same as you always imagine yourself. You follow a moving, dark strange man in linear (like the river) pursuit for six weeks along arctic mountains and rivers and an endless re-crossing of tracks and what else can you expect to see?

Some of the men who took part in that Albert Johnson pursuit cannot bear ever to talk about it; some can talk a little, but none of them will *do* it again; they refuse to repeat that story. There were three Loucheux Indians in that posse on the Eagle River on February 17, 1932: Johnny Moses,

Peter Alexis and Lazarus Sittichinli. Only Sittichinli is still alive; in fact, in 1987 he is the last man left of the entire hunt. The last white man, airplane mechanic Jack Owen, died in St. Albert outside Edmonton in 1985; he was flying Wop May's Bellanca, circling over the Eagle River while the great pilot himself was taking pictures of the shoot-out like a regular tourist.

Lazarus Sittichinli lives with his wife in a small red house in Aklavik two blocks from Albert Johnson's grave and across the street from the Anglican Hospital and the Anglican Church. He opens the door to me whom he has never seen or heard of: a tiny dark shrunken man, a few hairs bristle on his face, oddly powerful hands still with heavy horn-like nails. He walks to the kitchen table supporting himself on a four-point walker; he gestures for me to sit down. He is ninety-seven years old and he says it was he who lifted Johnson up out of the hole he had dug in the snow on the Eagle River, and turned him over so they could look at him. Peter Alexis and Karl Gardlund, who had been shooting from the same side of the river as Sittichinli, had advanced with him. Behind them came trader Frank Jackson and the police inspector.

"You know this man?" the inspector asked.

Alexis said, "I never know him."

In the warm house Mrs. Sittichinli sits dozing in a soft chair while the old man tells me that whole story again. Without prompting, as easily as if it had happened yesterday and acting out all the parts, changing voices, his brown hands shape the story in air and I know it so well I see and hear only the details that no one else can ever give me, the particularities which will disappear when this amazing Lazarus dies a year later: "Johnson he had a bullet cut all across his belly. He had no grub, he was eating spruce gum and whiskey jack. He had a string with a rag tied on it in the barrel of his 30-30 to keep out the snow so it wouldn't clog up and explode and he would jerk the string out and clean the barrel and shoot like that just about all the same motion. He was down there behind his big pack and I got down and lifted him up and turned him over. He didn't weigh nothing for a man, not as much as a big dog."

I mostly watch Lazarus' high-boned face move, shift in his slightly off-beat English; or his ancient wife, a soft mound breathing, her moosehide moccasins criss-crossed by thongs under her long cotton dress. They have been married for seventy-six years and twelve of their fourteen children have already died. But there are plenty of grand-children and great- and great-great-grandchildren around; one of them comes in to start supper. "My one son he marry a Husky," he laughs, and it takes me a moment to realize he means "Inuit" or "Inuvaluit" as the Mackenzie Inuit call themselves. Aklavik was the place of meeting between the Loucheux (or Kutchin) Indians and the Inuvaluit — they were always nervous, suspicious of each other, they were traditional enemies — and I ask him, "Do you Indians hunt beluga whales now?" but he says no, they never did. He never liked muktuk (whale blubber), he liked hunting caribou at the river crossings and sheep, lots of Dahl sheep in the mountains. "I'm always lucky hunting," he says. "All the men from town here always follow me hunting in the Richardson Mountains, sheep. All my life we live on hunting and trapping, we always live in the bush. Living like that."

"Could you do it, working as special constable for the police and live in the bush?"

"I never did after that," he says. "I quit, then."

So then I can ask him why. He is tired now and clearing his throat of phlegm, his toothless jaws moving sometimes as if he were eating Loucheux words which my Canadian ear could not understand anyway, though I should be able to see them in his hands and eyes. The story is long but he wants to tell it long, how he drove his dog-team back then from the Eagle River through fog over the mountains after four days and the inspector, whom May had flown in with the badly wounded Hersey and Johnson's body, told him to take a holiday after so much hard work on the two-month patrol. He was earning only seventy-five dollars a month. But next morning the inspector (Lazarus never calls him Eames or Alex; he names him only by function) was at his door as usual, telling him to haul in four tall trees for flag poles. Several other things happened then but now Lazarus shifts erect at the table, his black eyes suddenly fierce, bright. "I was mad," he says. "I tell him I'm not working no more. I quit now, you break your word, I break my word. I go home. A little later the inspector he come to my house. 'Why you quit?' 'You're asking too much.' 'No, no, you stay with us.' 'No.' 'Well, be the town police then.' 'No,' I say, 'I won't police my own people, that's no good.' So I go home and I stay quit."

Like every storyteller in the North he has acted all the parts as he speaks them, his voice changing to suit authority or obedience or anger. But at times there was something else in his tone; something like the man in Old Crow remembering his uncle Johnny Moses who had followed the twisting, spiralling river of Johnson's self-mocking flight almost as far as Lazarus Sittichinli, and who had been there when Lazarus lifted that frost-mutilated, starved body out of the snow. "I said I have a good place on the Husky River," this ancient man tells me in his strange, abstracted tone. "Good trapping. And I work sometimes in the hospital. But not the police."

William Nerysoo speaks the same way. He is ninety-four years old, living alone in a one-room house surrounded by Fort McPherson. He took no part in the six-week hunt; he was the man who originally reported to the police that he believed Johnson was disturbing his traps and that report started it all. When I visit him in 1983 the first thing he says to me is, "I won't tell you anything about that. Everybody comes here and asks me, I go to the store and the little boys yell after me, 'Hey, Mad trapper! Mad trapper!' I don't tell you anything." "Okay," I say, "Okay." What else can I say? His neighbor William Snowshoe comes into the little house then, we talk about the caribou of the Porcupine River herd moving north beyond the Richardson Mountains to their spring calving grounds, and suddenly Nerysoo says, "Maybe I'll tell you one thing." So he does that, and then we talk about the caribou some more and suddenly he says again, "Maybe I'll tell you one thing." After an afternoon he has told me his whole story and though I will not repeat it, his tone and his rectangular, gaunt face and his gentle insistent return to that trapline are telling me more than his words about that trap and the fatal report he once made because it was his place and his living. What is it about these strong, fierce-eyed old men? They are, in Chekhovian terms, "insisting so strongly on preserving someone's personal secret." It seems they are, for that insistence, the most civilized of people. I asked Lazarus Sittichinli about digging up that famous grave down his street.

"I don't like that," he says. "There are people who do all kinds of things to themselves — if you want some fingerprints, take theirs. But no digging. Johnson, he had enough suffering. Leave him alone."

Alone with his locked, his unlockable, secret. His told and untold, his trackable and untrackable, story. The long river of his flight is as obvious and as opaque as the Peel on which he first appeared, the gigantic Mackenzie whose opaqueness it somewhere, indecipherably, enters. Or as Peter Guy would have it in *But We Are Exiles*, the Mackenzie riverboat pilot with "eleven hundred miles of river in his head," on that river "a man is defined free from the terrors of human relationship. . . . an order maintained as precariously as that maintained by the hands on the wheel. The chaos held in check. . . . " In check perhaps, but it of course remains there, lurking.

These Indian men remember their roles in the hunt for that man who defended his aloneness with such single-minded and truly horrifying intensity with no joy, with no recalled heroism. At the same time they are themselves the farthest thing from being loners. White people like Albert Johnson or Peter Guy appearing from somewhere in southern Canada may be that — leave them alone — but a Loucheux or Inuit loner seems merely incredible. It is a contradiction by very concept. All Indians and Inuit have extended families that stretch far beyond children in all possible directions of cousins and nieces and parents and multiple adoptions and in-laws. No native of the Arctic seems to live as a solitary; everyone lives in a community and in any one community everyone, except for the few resident whites, is related to everyone else. Further, when any community has an occasion or festival, all those extended relations from all the other communities within a day's flying will arrive by chartered plane to help in the celebration.

When they do that they tell each other their continuing stories even as they live any number of new ones: stories here are a construct of actions and spoken words by means of which humanity remembers.

And this oral storytelling, so refined and perfected by millenia of practice, is the very affirmation of their non-aloneness: the storyteller and the poet/singer presuppose a community of listeners, otherwise nothing can be told. One may read a book alone (in fact most of us prefer that) but one cannot tell a story alone, which is why any language changes so drastically when it moves from oral to written form. Now the most minimal and therefore most powerful word, spoken or written, about any human being is *name*, and anyone who can hide that goes beyond secret into enigma, that is, into intentional and impenetrable obscurity. There is then no story to tell and the original people of the Canadian Arctic living in tiny communities on the immense polar landscape find such a refusal of story especially strange, disturbing, puzzling as only an oral, communal people can. But they respect it. Leave him alone. The story is there but there is no story to tell. Or as William Nerysoo tells me, under most conditions I won't tell you the part of the story I know. Yet he is too much a person of his people and his landscape ultimately to refuse it; all I have to do is be there and wait long enough.

When I visit William Nerysoo again four years later I do not talk to him about Johnson at all, and that very fact helps me comprehend a further dimension of the landscape of story in his life. Because Nerysoo *is* a great storyteller; he tells me a collection of his stories translated into English is with an editor and they will, hopefully soon, be well and properly published. From behind the curtain of his bedroom he brings out the manuscript and lets me glance through it. There are many brief stories: one called "Rat and Beaver — Changing Tails" begins: "This story started over a hundred years ago when beaver was a man. Families of beaver. . . . " Now somewhere before 1800 David Thompson heard and recorded the ancient Cree stories of the beavers being an ancient people that lived on dry land, though the Cree remembered them as being always beaver, not humans, so of course I want to read this Loucheux story. The old man laughs aloud:

"How much will you pay me, to read it?"

"How much do you want?" I ask.

"Two thousand dollars!"

Then we both laugh and talk of other things. It is exactly the same experience the Danish explorer Knud Rasmussen had in 1921 when he asked a Netsilik Inuit shaman to sing him his song so he could record it; the shaman wanted a rifle in exchange or he would not sing it.

Songs, stories are beyond value; they are the memory and wisdom of a people, the particular individual rivers of the sea of life which constitutes us all. And when you hide that, when you insist the river of your life is as opaque as the Mackenzie or Peel, you are defying the ancient assertion of that sea: you still do have a story (you cannot *not* have a story because you had a mother, you had a place and time when you were born, you have moved because you are alive), but if you persist so absolutely with silence, motionless silence even unto death, then we will respect your refusal of your own story. We will leave you alone. Though we will continue to tell what little we do know because that is the only way human life continues. The plains Blackfoot story of how death came into the world expresses this understanding most cogently:

Old Man covered the plains with grass for the animals to feed on. He marked off a piece of ground, and in it he made to grow all kinds of roots and berries — camas, wild carrots, wild turnips, sweet-root, bitter-root, sarvis berries, wild turnips, bull berries, cherries, plums, and rosebuds. He put trees in the ground. He put all kinds of animals on the ground. . . .

One day Old Man determined that he would make a woman and a child; so he formed them both — the woman and the child, her son — of clay. After he had moulded the clay in human shape, he said to the clay, "You must be people," and then he covered it up and left it, and went away. The next morning he went to the place and took the covering off, and saw that the clay shapes had changed a little. The second morning there was still more change, and the third still more. The fourth morning he went to the place, took the covering off, looked at the images, and told them to rise and walk; and they did so. They walked down to the river with their Maker, and then he told them that his name was *Na'pi*, Old Man.

As they were standing by the river, the woman said to him, "How is it? Will we always live, will there be no end to it?" He said: "I have never thought of that. We will have to decide it. I will take this buffalo chip and throw it in the river. If it floats, when people die, in four days they will become alive again; they will die for only four days. But if it sinks, there will be an end to them." He threw the chip into the river, and it floated. The woman turned and picked up a stone, and said: "No, I will throw this stone in the river; if it floats we will always live, if it sinks people must die, that they may always be sorry for each other" [i.e., that their surviving friends may always remember them]. The woman threw the stone into the water, and it sank. "There," said Old Man, "you have chosen. There will be an end to them."

It was not many nights after, that the woman's child died, and she cried a great deal for it. She said to Old Man: "Let us change this. The law that you first made, let that be a law." He said: "Not so. What is made law must be law. We will undo nothing that we have done. The child is dead, but it cannot be changed. People will have to die."

That is how we came to be people. It is he who made us.

There is an overwhelming doubleness to death: it brings sorrow and at the same time it makes possible the story which is our memory of the dead. But that is also death's true and abiding horror. "Who will remember our dead?" cries the woman Shanawdithit in 1837, the last person alive of her Beothuk people. "Who will remember us?" The ultimate horror of genocide is the final disappearance of a particular human memory, that is, of one human story. The tall red Beothuks of Newfoundland chased and killed like animals in the nineteenth century, the handsome Salliq Inuit of Southampton Island wiped out by white disease in the twentieth — there is not one of them left who can remember. Annihilation indeed. But it seems the peoples of the Arctic respect individuals even in that; they will allow you annihilation, if you use up your one life to insist on it.

For their own part, however, they are consummate storytellers and they prefer happier endings. In 1836 Richard King recorded the human creation story of the Yellow-knife/Chipewyan Indians:

Old Soul, renowned warrior in his youthful days, freely and cheerfully related to us the tradition current among his tribe with regard to the creation, being in substance as follows: — The Indian did not pretend to give an opinion in what way man got into the world, but commenced by saying he made his first appearance during the summer months, when the berries were abundant on the earth, upon which his subsistence entirely depended. As soon as the winter set in, the depth of snow inconvenienced him in so great a degree, that in accordance with the trite adage, "necessity is the mother of invention," he at once conceived the formation of the show-shoe. After the lapse of a short time the birchen frames were perfected; but as he could not net them, for that was a woman's work, they remained unfinished in his lodge; from which circumstance his labour was very much increased, and the chance of gaining a subsistence became every day more precarious. One day, on returning to his hut, a noise as if some one was working at the snow-shoe frames attracted his notice; and upon a nearer approach, a wood-partridge [i.e. ptarmigan] flew from the opening at the top, which at that time he paid little regard to. The succeeding day he sallied forth on another hunting excursion; and having remained out until quite dark, his attention was suddenly drawn towards his hut by the appearance of volumes of smoke issuing from it. Returning home with all speed, he perceived a wood-partridge again make its escape; and on entering the tent, found his snow-shoes more than half netted, and carefully placed beyond the reach of a fire that was blazing inside. Suspecting the partridge had effected all this, though in what manner could not be divined, he determined to secure it if at all practicable; and with this view the roof of the tent was carefully closed prior to his departure on another hunting trip which he took a few days afterwards. It occurred to him that by returning earlier than usual the bird might be taken by surprise; he therefore approached the door of the tent with the utmost caution, and was fortunate enough by that means to cut off the retreat of the partridge, which instantly became metamorphosed into a young wife; whence the world soon became peopled.

Truly a beautiful story to be told "freely and cheerfully," by the rightly named person: Old Soul. When in the long winter of 1820-21 Robert Hood painted Green Stockings webbing a snowshoe, was he listening to this first story of man's and woman's creation? He would certainly have recognized how the almost wistful longing for "helpmeet" in Genesis is here fulfilled without any deception or accusation or guilt, or eternal exile from a garden. Living in a climate as harsh as any on earth, these "primitives" emphasize not individual temptation and disobedience, but complementarity.

As for Richard King, it is obvious he can much more easily record in English the ways of a man with a bird than the ways of a man with a woman: from vivid detail his story stutters down into generality. And he does not seem to comprehend Old Soul's further story of the confusion of tongues:

For several generations after the creation there existed only one language; but, owing to an unfortunate circumstance, that harmony was soon destroyed. A number of children assembled together, having exhausted all the games they had been accustomed to play, were at a loss how they could further amuse themselves. Having observed and participated in the joy that invariably spread itself through the whole camp on their parents killing and cutting up the several animals of the chace, they agreed among themselves to go through the ceremony in play. One of the juveniles was accordingly hung after the manner of strangling the deer when caught in a snare, until he ceased to live, and the body immediately afterwards divided into several portions. Each, laden with a share, proceeded to the respective tents of their parents, and related the droll game they had been playing. The horrid deed so shocked them, that they were not only utterly confounded, but rendered incapable of comprehending each other, and in consequence separated into far-distant countries.

King does not seem to recognize this as a singular parallel to the Genesis Cain and Abel/Tower of Babel stories. But again, how humanely softened. The first sibling is killed by children at play imitating the necessary adult behavior with animals (the northern people in their stories never make much distinction between humans and animals) — not, as in Genesis, because of competition, jealousy and hatred. The language confusion also is not a judgment of a divinity angered by people overreaching themselves in pride; it results from individual abhorrence of an inhumane act. Such a story the pre-Victorian Christian Richard King labels as a "rude idea"!

Fortunately today northern people are themselves telling their stories. One of the first to tell his own story at length in English was Anthony Apakark Thrasher of Paulatuk, Northwest Territories, in a book called *Thrasher . . . Skid Row Eskimo*. He tells of his family traditions:

Story telling was a part of life in the North. My brothers and I were always competing to tell the best story. But we were no match for our grandfather. He was the greatest of them all. As he talked, he would light his pipe, and smoke "Old Chum" tobacco. Then he would pick up his drum, and sing. He would sing of Herschel Island in the Arctic Ocean, and tell of times that were good. He would sing of happiness after a successful whale hunt, about the big dances people used to have, of his young days, and his women, and of the medicine men of old.

The grandfather Tony Thrasher speaks of here is Billy Thrasher, called "Thrasher" after the name of the whaling ship he was born on, a legendary man of the North who was, like many Inuit today, partly white. Billy's grandson goes on to tell the story of how he experienced his father's death:

One night, when I was in Tuk[toyaktuk] in 1962, I thought I saw two shadows making motions for me to follow. I was staying with my sister, Mary, and my four nieces. I asked them if they could see these two things calling me. I had a strange feeling and I told Mary, "Dad is calling. Something is wrong with him."

I took a snowmobile to Inuvik [nearly two hundred kilometres over ice and tundra] and found my father had died of a heart attack.

Thrasher drinks heavily, gets arrested for breaking and entering and is jailed for three months. He continues:

My dad's death, my new criminal record, the VD, and my trouble with girls made me head back to my home village of Paulatuk.

In late fall, I went out to my trapline and made a mistake on the [sea] ice. I forgot to watch the wind shifting from northeast to southwest, and I found myself stranded on an ice floe in a storm. I had thirteen dogs and only a few fish. It was hard to see in the storm and I made a snow house and waited. The first night was not bad. I managed to catch two seals and feed the dogs, but two weeks later I was still out there. One night the wind was bad and I lost four dogs. When I awakened, they were frozen to the ice. By the time the fourth week arrived, I was hungry and my dogs were starving. Two more dogs froze on the ice and I cut them up and fed them to the remaining dogs, and ate some myself. It was like bear meat.

I now had seven dogs left. On the thirty-first day, the wind took me somewhere close to Pearce Point. But the weather was still bad and I couldn't tell just how close to shore we came. My blankets were frozen stiff. I had a stove with one gallon of coal oil. One of the dogs was frozen on one side, and the hair came off. He was one that had worked especially hard to help me and I didn't have the heart to shoot him. I made a snow house for him and left him some scrap bones.

That day I almost gave up hope. I was very tired and I thought if I fall asleep, I'm done. I remember my dad telling me never to give up. If you have a will, you have hope.

Finally, the storm let up a little. Thirty miles away I could see the Paulatuk Hills. My heart leapt. I helped my six dogs to pull the sled, and made it there in nine hours. I had a ten dollar Timex wristwatch from the Hudson's Bay Company, and I used it as a compass. But no one was around in Paulatuk. There was an old oil stove in the Mission church. I entered and lit it. The old Father won't mind, I thought. I put my dogs inside the covered porch and found some cornmeal and seal oil, and fed them and myself. I also found some coffee and some of Father's wine. I thawed it out, drank only one cup, and put the bottle back.

The next day I continued my journey, stopping at Bennett Point to camp. It was a beautiful moonlit night. The following morning I was on my way again, and that night I camped at Letty Harbour. The next day I got a few miles from Cape Parry, and my dogs gave up. I was helping them but they were too tired, so I tied them up. I had a little piece of fish, and I cut it up and gave it to them.

It was blowing hard, and I made a little snow house. It was just big enough so that I could sit in it and kneel down. For the first time I prayed to God to help me make it home.

The wind dropped. I picked up my rifle and left the dogs. I figured I would get them later, but now they needed rest. I was weak, and three miles of walking seemed like many more, and it took me about six hours. My journey home had taken me one month and five days. Most of this time my people thought I was fishing. On the day I arrived home a plane was going out to look for me. I was quite a sight, my parka and blankets were stiff with ice, and it took nearly half an hour by the stove to thaw my parka out so I could get it off.

I was lucky.

I have known many people who never came back. I recall one hunter who went out looking for caribou, and his body was never found. We think he must have rolled himself up in raw caribou skin. If you wrap the skin around you, even in twenty-below weather, you are stuck in there for good, to starve. The skin freezes hard and you can't get out.

There are all kinds of ways of dying out there. Some people get tired, and go to sleep, and never wake up. Freezing makes you sleepy. There is loss of pain when your brain starts to freeze. I have felt that way more than once.

Now the story of physically and psychically surviving (the latter, it seems to me, must be the more difficult of the two) alone and motionless on an ice pan for thirty-six days is not the only experience people can have in the Arctic, any more than the experience of surviving on skid row with drunkenness, violence, prostitution and dreadful debilitating scavenging and crime is the only story to be told about large Canadian cities. But they are only too possible; for Thrasher they are more than possible, they are perhaps inevitable in the life he has come to live, and he tells these stories also in *Skid Row Eskimo* with a devastating frankness. In doing so, one of his nephews at Paulatuk tells me, he hurt some people in that community because "they were talked about without permission." One's story is rarely only one's own; if you tell yours, others will be involved. What storyteller has not been made aware of that? So eleven years after he told part of his, Tony Thrasher lives, somehow, across the North Saskatchewan River from me in Edmonton; not in Paulatuk or Tuktoyaktuk or Holman where almost all of his family is. Perhaps he wants to spare them his further story; perhaps Albert Johnson wanted the same.

There is, then, something to be said for Johnson's refusal. And death continues to hide him. Experts disagree about whether the permafrost at Aklavik is strong enough to preserve his body so well that fingerprints could still be taken. "Hell," one Aklavik resident tells me, "I've lived here for twelve years and I've seen the Mackenzie flood the graveyard so bad there were bones floating around. There's nothing left of him." A moving graveyard? The river aiding and abetting a secret again? Besides, the territorial governor explained to me, between 1932-33 three suicides had been buried around Johnson and now, even if the bodies were well preserved, no one would know exactly which body was whose. Ironically the iconoclast Johnson, who in life refused to live near anyone, in death is protected by what he would have considered a crowd. In any case, soon after the April 27 announcement a petition against the disinterment was signed by more people than actually live in Aklavik. It seems that historian Dick North with his implacable white man's obsession to know is not going to get his clinching evidence. Johnson remains an enigmatic secret. Perhaps fifty-five years is enough to leave him there; to leave him *alone*.

A further question: how could Green Stockings' and Robert Hood's daughter remain for decades such a secret to the English? In 1820 George Back rivalled Hood for the Indian woman's favour, and twice after Hood's death he returned to the country of the Yellowknives: once as Franklin's lieutenant down the Mackenzie (1825-27) and once in command of his own highly successful expedition (1833-35) when he mapped every inch of the sprawling Back River from its beginning (or end) in Sussex Lake across the tundra to the ocean. In 1826 at Great Bear Lake he paints a picture of Broad Face, probably one of Green Stockings' husbands when he first met her; in July 1834, both he and his lieutenant King verify that they meet Green Stockings herself at the Muskox Rapids on the Back River. She is "surrounded by family" — children only, no husband(s) mentioned. If Hood's daughter is alive, she is in that "surround," moving, unhidden. Why does Doctor King, who would have been only too happy to obtain a hard fact that would embarrass Back and the earlier Franklin expedition, not mention this girl? Does he not know what he is seeing? He who is so quick in recognition does not recognize Hood in any of the children? Back, for obvious reasons of loyalty and personal reputation, will say nothing either to King or in his published narrative. And the Yellowknives are, as always, too careful of another's story to speak, though this particular small river flows so integrally from their own large story sea into that of the English.

I have been contemplating arctic Canada more as water than as land: the sea, the rivers, ice, cloud, fog, an occasional lake. The people I have talked about moved across the landscape largely by means of water: the two Franklin expeditions, Back and King, the Yellowknives, Green Stockings and her linear husbands and children, Albert Johnson, the men who pursued him, Tony Thrasher. One might deduce from my considerations that all human beings, certainly all whites, made their entry into the arctic landscape by means of water and that for most of the last four hundred years of arctic encounter the whites have not wanted land there at all. They want water, and not in its peculiar, inconvenient at best and deadly at worst, mix of ice/fog/liquid either. They want nothing except liquid water so they can get past the land because they do not want to stop in the Arctic at all: they merely want it to be a convenient passage to another place altogether.

And the Arctic has never cooperated; it is too much itself to be merely a means for anything. The image of water I have used thus far certainly corroborates such a deduction. It also affirms the idea that movement within a landscape, whether on water or occasionally land, can be seen in the linear image of water moving down to the sea, or, if you grant me my original reversed conceit, of the rivers being the tentacles of the protean sea reaching over the land. In other words, the movement (life) of human beings is always analogous to the line water draws upon land.

I would like to re-affirm this identification of ocean and river and life by quoting a lyric, the personal song of the Igloolik Inuit shaman Uvavnuk. Both Knud Rasmussen and Peter Freuchen record this beautiful lyric, and it will serve here as an introduction to my concluding chapter when I will tell the story of how Uvavnuk received this song, how it changed her life and made her a great shaman. She sings:

> The great sea
> Has set me adrift:
> It moves me as a small plant
>   in the running river,
> Earth and the mighty weather
> Move me,
> Storm through me,
> Have carried me away,
> And I tremble with joy.

III

IN YOUR OWN HEAD

Wishing to begin to walk,
Wishing to begin to walk,
Wishing to begin to walk,
To Kuluksuk I began to walk.

Higilaq, "Dance Song," 1900

Since I have spoken at length about river, sea and movement as a possible way to understanding, to developing an appreciation for Canada's Arctic landscape, the personal lyric by the Igloolik shaman Uvavnuk is particularly apt. Here is the poem again in a slightly different translation from that by Rasmussen:

Moved

The great sea stirs me.
The great sea sets me adrift,
It sways me like the weed
On a river stone.

The sky's height stirs me.
The strong wind blows through my mind.
It carries me with it
So I shake with joy.

As Robin McGrath has pointed out, Inuit "oral poetry has the reputation of being the best primitive literature known to man." At the same time she notes that in English we are three removes from its true genius: "we read it rather than hear it, we read it in translation, and it must be read without the benefit of [its traditional] musical accompaniment." Inuit oral poetry is too enormous and complex a subject to discuss here: perhaps it would suffice to tell the story of how this song came to Uvavnuk "when the spirit of a meteor entered her." Knut Rasmussen recounts that

Uvavnuk had gone out outside the hut one winter evening to make water. It was a particularly dark evening, as the moon was not visible. Then suddenly a glowing ball of fire appeared in the sky and it came rushing down to earth straight toward her. She could have gotten up and fled, but before she could pull up her breeches, the ball of fire struck her and entered into her. At the same moment she perceived that all within her grew light, and she lost consciousness. But from that moment also she became a great shaman.

Peter Freuchen tells the story of Uvavnuk a little differently: she ran inside her igloo and immediately fell down senseless with joy. When she recovered, she sang the song to her astounded companions.

Not only do the images in the poem coelesce; it is also clear that the meteor and the song and the great shaman power come upon Uvavnuk as she is urinating in the darkness, that is, at that moment during the polar night when she is joining the fluid stream of her body to the winter snow and ice which covers the earth. As the Cree chief Big Bear says in a similar situation, she is at that moment "embracing the whole earth in one flowing stream." The waters of the earth — the sea — are the source of all life: according to Copper Inuit myth the goddess Nuliajuk (by other tribes called Taleelayo or Sedna) lives at the bottom of the sea and is the mother of all animals, both marine (seal, walrus, polar bear) and land (caribou, muskox). So this gift of song from water and sky is power indeed; no wonder Uvavnuk became a great shaman. We can easily understand then that when, out of the sea, Europeans first appeared to the Inuit, they were both feared and defied and befriended and almost worshipped by them: whatever the sea brought could not be completely alien, though the experience of it might very well be frightening or catastrophic as the visitations of Nuliajuk often were.

The first detailed record of Inuit encounters with the English is given in 1575 by George Best in "The First Voyage of Discovery under the Conduct of Marten Frobisher, Generall." Frobisher sails his single ship the *Gabriel* (a second has returned to England intimidated by the ice) into what he, with the becoming modesty of all great explorers, calls "Frobishers Streytes, lyke as Magellanus at the Southweast ende of the world, hauing discoured the passage to the South Sea (where America is deuided from the continente of that lande whiche lyeth vnder the South Pole) and called the same straites Magellanus streightes."

Frobisher had not, of course, discovered anything quite so momentous as had Magellan; he was sailing in neither strait nor passage, rather into the very long bay on the fifth largest island in the world: Frobisher Bay on Baffin Island (then not yet named). Going ashore he saw "mightie deere" and also "signe where fire had bin made," and shortly after from

vpon the toppe of a hill, he perceiued a number of small things fléeting in the Sea a farre off, whyche hée supposed to be Porposes, or Ceales, or some kinde of strange fishe: but comming nearer, he discouered them to be men, in small boates made of leather. And before he could discende downe from the hyll, certain of those people had almost cut off his boate from him, hauing stollen secretely behinde the rocks for that purpose, where he spéedily hasted to his boate, and bent himselfe to his Holbert [ie. halberd, a speared axe with a seven-foot handle], and narrowly escaped the daunger, and saued his bote. Afterwards, he had sundry conferences with them, and they came aborde his ship, and brought him Salmon and raw fleshe and fishe, and gréedily deuoured the same before our mens faces. And to shewe their agilitie, they tryed many maisteries, vpon the ropes of the ship, after our Mariners fashion, [it seems obvious from this that they had encountered whites before, perhaps whalers or Newfoundland fishermen] and appeared to be verie strong of theyr armes, and nimble of their bodies. They exchaunged coates of Ceale, and Beares skinnes, and suche like, with oure men, and receiued belles, loking glasses, and other toyes in recompence thereof againe. After great curtesie, and manye méetings, our Mariners, contrarie to their Captaines dyrection, began more easily to trust them, and fiue of our men going a shoare, were by them intercepted with their boate, and were neuer since hearde of to this day againe. So that the Captaine being destitute of boate, barke, and al company, had scarcely sufficient number to conduct back his bark againe. He coulde nowe neither conuey himselfe a shore to rescue his men (if he had bin able) for want of a boate, and again, the subtile traytours, were so warie, as they would after that neuer come within our mens danger. The Captaine (notwithstanding) desirous to bring some token from thence, of his being there, was greatly discontented, that he had not before apprehended some of them. And therefore to deceiue the deceiuers, he wrought a prettie pollicie, for knowing well how they greatly delighted in our toyes, and specially in belles, he rang a pretie Lowbel, making wise that he would giue him the same that would come and fetch it. And bycause they would not come within his daunger [power or reach] for feare, he flung one bell vnto them, which of purpose he threw short, that it might fal into the sea and be lost. And to make them more gréedie of the matter, he rang a lowder bell, so that in the ende one of them came neare the ship side, to receiue the bell, which when he thought to take at the Captaines hand, he was therby taken himself. For the Captain being redily prouided, let the bel fal, & cought the man fast, & plucked him with maine force, boate and al into his bark, out of the Sea: Whervpon when he founde himself in captiuitie, for very choller & disdain he bit his tong in twayne within his mouth: notwithstanding, he died not therof, but liued vntill he came in Englande, and then he died, of colde which he had taken at Sea.

Nowe with this newe pray (whiche was a sufficiente witnesse of the Captaines farre and tedious trauell towardes the vnknowne partes of the worlde, as did well appeare by this strange Infidel, whose like was neuer séen, red, nor harde of before, and whose language was neyther knowne nor vnderstoode of anye) the saide Captaine Frobisher returned homeward, and arriued in England, in August folowing .An. 1576.

Frobisher sailed north by west again on May 25, 1577, intent to recover his five lost men and progress further up the Northwest Passage he believed he had entered. The black rocks with which he returned and which he and his backers mistakenly assumed contained gold need not detain us; the rocks are merely one of a long list of false treasures with which the Arctic has mocked its would-be exploiters. His third voyage a year later established an English colony on Baffin Island eight years before Grenville's attempt to colonize Roanoke Island, Virginia, but all Frobisher's energetic colony achieved was hauling fifteen hundred more tons of worthless rock to England. The backers were so disgusted with this unnecessary geology when its worthlessness was at last correctly analysed that it was dumped into the sea and so lost forever to subsequent scientific analysis. In any case, in 1577 Frobisher reached the same spot on Frobisher Bay (Strait then) and found plenty of torn clothing as evidence of his sailors' presence there, but the "savages" would not reveal them to him. They were alternately friendly and violent, and the Elizabethan sailors were nothing loath to test their blunderbusses and crossbows and halberds against arrows and spears and harpoons; after all, before Frobisher sailed to the Northwest Passage he sailed as a pirateer for Queen Elizabeth against the Spanish galleons hauling gold from Central America. Sometime in August sailors and "savages" on Baffin Island fought a major battle in which the "people of the country" (they had no English name as yet) proved themselves very resourceful indeed:

And desperately retorning vpon our men, resisted them manfullye in their landing, so long as theyr arrows and dartes lasted, & after gathering vp those arrows which our men shot at them, yea, and plucking our arrowes out of their bodies, encountred afresh againe, and maintained their cause, vntil both weapons & life vtterly failed them. And when they founde they were mortally wounded, being ignorant what mercy meaneth [and the English apparently incapable of demonstrating it], with deadly furie they cast themselues headlong from off the rocks into the sea, least perhaps their enimies shoulde receiue glorie or praye of their dead carcasses, for they supposed vs be like to be Canibales, or eaters of mans flesh. In this conflict one of our men was dangerouslie hurt in the bellie with one of their arrowes, and of them were slayne fiue or sixe. The rest by flight escaped among the Rockes, sauing two women, whereof the one being old and ougly, oure men thought she had bin a Diuell or some Witch, & therfore let hir go: the other being yong, & combred with a sucking childe at hir backe, hiding hirselfe behinde the rocks, was espied by one of oure men, who supposing she had bin a man, shot through the heare of hir head, & pierced through the childs arme [the child would have been hanging in the hood on her back], wherevpon she cried out, & was taken, & our Surgeon meaning to heale hir childs arme, applyed salues thervnto. But she not acquainted with such kinde of surgerie, plucked those salues away, & by continuall licking with hir owne tongue, not muche vnlike oure dogges, healed vppe the childes arme.

They had earlier captured a man, and Best continues:

Hauing now got a woman captiue for the comforte [any woman will, of course, do] of our man, we broughte them both togither, and euery man with silence desired to beholde the manner of their méeting and entertaynement, the whiche was more worth the beholding, than can be well expressed by writing. At theyr first encountring, they behelde each the other very wistly [i.e., silent, close attention, intently] a good space, withoute spéeche or worde vttered, with greate change of coloure and countenaunce, as though it seemed, the greefe and disdeyne of their captiuitie had taken away the vse of their tongs and vtterance: the woman at the first verie suddaynely, as though she disdeyned or regarded not the man, turned away, and beganne to sing [her death song?], as though she minded another matter: but being agayne broughte togyther, the man brake vp the silence first, and with sterne and stayed countenaunce, beganne to tell a long solemne tale to the woman, wherevnto she gaue good hearing, and interrupted him nothing, till he had finished, & afterwards, being growen into more familiar acquayntance by speech, were turned togither, so that (I thinke) the one would hardly haue liued, without the comfort of the other. And, for so muche as we coulde perceiue, albeit they liued continually togither, yet did they neuer vse as man and wife, though the woman spared not to do all necessarie things that apperteyned to a good huswife indifferently for them both, as in making cleane their Cabin, and euery other thing that apperteyned to his ease: ... Only I thinke it worth the noting the continencie of them both, for the man would neuer shift himselfe, except he had firste caused the woman to depart out of his Cabin, and they both were most shamefast, least anye of their priuie parts should bée discouered, eyther of themselves or any other body.

One assumes the Elizabethans, since they found this so noteworthy, had no such delicacy of toilet manners among themselves. Especially sailors on a very small ship on a very long voyage.

The people of the country thus violently stolen from their native land no more saw it again than the five sailors who ventured among them to trade contrary to their commander's orders. Not that people brought from the new world for display were unknown in Europe. The great Columbus himself forcibly brought ten natives of Hispaniola back to Spain on his very first voyage; six of them survived it to be baptized (forcibly?) in Barcelona and three of those lived long enough to return to their native land with Columbus on his second voyage (1494) where two of them escaped. The admiral, however, returned to Spain with thirty more natives, presumably to improve his average of deaths and escapes, and immediately sold all of them as slaves in Seville. In fact, by 1496 various Spanish sea

captains had brought more than fourteen hundred Amerin-
dians to Spain as slaves. The first North American native
arrived in England in 1502, brought there by Sebastian Cabot
from Newfoundland; Stow's *Chronicle* reports that "these
men were clothed in beasts skins, and eat raw flesh,
but . . . two of them were seen in the Kings court at Westmin-
ster two yeeres after clothed like Englishmen, and could not
be discerned from Englishmen."

Frobisher's Inuit captives seventy-five years later were
not nearly so adaptable. The three Baffin Islanders were
stared at and painted (the pictures by John White are still in
the British Museum) and put through their paces for the
queen's and the public's amusement. Seyer's 1821 *History of
Bristol* recounts:

In the year 1578 a great ship of our Queen's called the *Aid* . . . came
into Kingroad from Cattaie, Martin Frobisher being captain, after
having attempted to find the Northwest passage to the East Indies,
China and Cattay. . . . They brought with them a man of that country called Callicho (al' Cally Chough) with his wife, called Ignorth,
and a child. They were savage people, clothed in Stag's skins, having no linen nor woollen at all, and fed only upon raw flesh: she
suckled her child, casting her breasts over her shoulders [I cannot
imagine how this is physiologically possible]. October 9th, he
rowed up and down the river, at the Back of Bristol, it being high
tide of sea, in a boat, the which was about fourteen feet long, made
of skins, in form like unto a large barge or trow, but sharp at both
ends, having but one round place for him to sit in; and as he rowed
up and down he killed a couple of ducks with his dart; and when
he had done he carried away the boat through the marsh on his
back. The like he did at the Weare, and at other places. Within one
month they all three died.

No doubt death made them even more popular. As Trinculo
remarks in Shakespeare's *The Tempest* (1610?) "When they
[the English] will not give a doit to relieve a lone beggar,
they will lay out ten to see a dead Indian."

We know nothing of what these people, or their coun-
tryman a year before them, thought or enjoyed or suffered in
their brief encounter with Elizabethan England; how often
they sang, or what they sang since human beings often give
voice to great passion by breaking into song, both in joy and
in grief. Their deaths were swift and inevitable. They were
already dead when they were torn from their land, a fact
Callicho and Ignorth undoubtedly recognized when they
greeted each other so solemnly while being stared at by
every sailor on board the monstrous English ship. What did
the baby sense of this violent dislocation? In the painted picture there is only its tiny face all but hidden in the hood, a
round cherub nestled against its mother's face. Our impossi-
bility of understanding their speech ensures their unending
silence. The baby's inarticulate awareness, the adults' song
or language locked within them; their secrets died with them
and are as lost as their bones buried without proper
ceremony by deadly aggressive people with incomprehensi-
ble and to them meaningless customs in a strange land to
which they were with such violence brought. Nearly four
centuries had to pass before we at last can read of an Inuit
view of an encounter with English sailors.

In 1948 L.A. Learmouth recorded, translated and published in *The Beaver* (and reprinted in Gedalof) the Netsilik
Inuit story which had been passed on for 120 years in their
oral memories. A man named Ohokto told how the native
people of the Boothia Peninsula in 1829 first met Sir John
Ross and the men of his ship frozen in the ice:

On a day in the middle of the winter many years ago, off the north
shore of Lord Mayor Bay, south Boothia, in the opening between
what is now known as Victory Harbour and Felix Harbour [across
the peninsula from the modern town of Spence Bay], a number of
Boothian (Netsilik) natives were out aglo hunting [breathing-hole

sealing] as was their habit, when one, Ableelooktook, wandered far to the south of where his companions were hunting, led by his hunting dog straining eagerly at its leash. In permitting the dog to lead him there, Ableelooktook believed the animal had scented a bear. But suddenly he pulled up short because what was that he saw ahead? — strange sight indeed — what appeared to be a house, but not such as he was familiar with, with smoke pouring from its roof and many human beings moving around in its vicinity.

Not knowing what this strange sight could mean, Ableelooktook was greatly frightened, and without delay took to his heels and made back to the snow village, situated well back in the bay, whose entrance lay between Felix and Victory Harbours. There he arrived as darkness set in, and just as his companions also returned from their hunting.

Soon he had told of his discovery, upon which the whole population of the village quickly gathered together in the large village dance house to discuss the matter. Here the principal Angekok [medicine man] donned his main belt of charms and his cape, made of pieces of white deer belly hide, and without delay got to work. He first took a large deerskin and pegged it to the west wall inside the dance house so as to leave the lower side resting partly on the floor. He then obtained a pair of deerskin pants from one of the men and carefully laid them out on the floor behind the deerskin curtain with legs pointing towards the back wall, then crawled in behind the curtain, ordered all kudlik [stone lamp] lights to be extinguished, and the seance was on.

In crawling in behind the curtain the Angekok was careful to follow the direction travelled by the sun and the moon, because they were all afraid, and only thus could contact be established with the spirits it was necessary to consult. To have crawled in behind the curtain in the opposite direction to that travelled by the sun and the moon would have offended the spirits and prevented them from coming to the aid of these sorely troubled people.

As the crowd of scared men, women and children huddled together and anxiously waited in the darkened dance house, the Angekok got in touch with his familiar spirits and through them with all the other spirits that mattered, who all trooped in behind the curtain one after the other. First came those of the Sun, Moon and stars, then that of the giant who lived in the mountains back of Pelly Bay, of Nulaiyuk who controls the spirits of the mammals of the sea, of the deer and the bear and so on, down to even the spirit

IN YOUR OWN HEAD

of the lowly tom cod!

When all the spirits had gathered together under the curtain, they informed the Angekok that the strangers seen by Ableelooktook were white men and that they would welcome a visit by the Eskimos. Then, to wind up, the spirits of the white men themselves arrived behind the curtain and invited all the Eskimos to visit their camp at Felix Harbour the following day.

Thus it was the entire population of the village turned out by daybreak the following morning and proceeded to Felix Harbour. When they came in sight of the house [the ship *Victory* under canvas covers and dismantled] they halted and sent forward Nalungituk to await the arrival of some of the white men who could be seen approaching without knives or spears or anything in their hands. Soon they were all on friendly terms with each other and moved over close to the house, where the boss of the white men came forward and greeted them.

After the second round of greeting was over, the boss [John Ross, presumably] enquired for the man who had been seen near the camp on the previous day as he wished to make him a present. Whereupon Ableelooktook stepped forward and went with him into the house. Once inside the boss handed him an ooloo, a woman's knife, which offended Ableelooktook, because he was a man and a great hunter. What did he want with a woman's knife? So he pointed to a hand saw which was hanging on a nail and indicated he would prefer that to the ooloo. This in turn made the boss angry, and he thereupon took the ooloo back from Ableelooktook, refused him the saw and chased him out of the house.

Afterwards the white men made presents of what appears to have been gun caps and what the Eskimos thought must be very small thimbles, and bullets which they afterwards used as sinkers for their fish jigging hooks, and thus ends the story of "Ableelooktook" as told by Ohokto.

It seems to me beyond question that this extraordinary seance in the village dance house, where the spirits speak so humanely and so true to the angekok, helps save the expedition. The fact is that, though Ross lost his ship to the ice, after four long years in the Arctic he managed to get back safely to England in 1833 with all but three of his men alive and well. Perhaps it was these very Inuit who of necessity taught him the crucial truth that to live in the Arctic as they had for millenia without scurvy, Ross and his men must eat fresh meat (preferably raw) and oil, not canned beef, hardtack, and rancid lime juice; a lesson which Sir John Franklin had not yet learned fifteen years later when he with his two ships disappeared forever. And for me the most beautiful element of all in this story is that not only did the familiar spirits of the angekok come to speak such humane wisdom to the people, the spirits of the Englishmen themselves "arrived behind the curtain and invited all the Eskimos to visit their camp." Isolated, frozen, forlorn, it is hard for us to imagine how much the whites must have been longing for some companionship, some trace of human life and warmth in the vast alien reaches of Lord Mayor Bay; consciously or unconsciously their spirits and the spirits of the Netsilik people spoke to each other before they ever met. Polar stillness particularly needs human companionship.

There is a further matter of history here, of northernness which we need to be clear about. The European entry into the western hemisphere and the Christian encounter with its native inhabitants was, generally speaking, violent. At the same time, the Europeans dragged all their national wars and hatreds onto this continent, wars both political and territorial (as between the French and the English), and commercial (as between the Hudson's Bay and the North West trading companies), and religious (Roman Catholic and Protestant). These imported conflicts often become all the more violent for the distance from "home" and "law" and "public opinion" at which they were carried on. But there was also plenty of violence and brutality and hatred native to North America. To speak of arctic Canada only: no more before than after Europeans arrived was there a great deal of "noble savage" paradise discernible here. Why in the 1820s did the usually docile Dogribs annihilate the Yellowknife tribe, the people that had saved the lives of all but one of the whites in the first Franklin expedition? Did the Yellow-knives, with their aggressive male wars of pillage, woman stealing and trade dominance, bring the Dogrib retaliation upon themselves?

In 1851 Dr. John Richardson records his story of how the Dogribs, who he writes "shrink from pain, show little daring," finally broke the spirits of their aggressive neighbours:

They [the Dogribs] do not meet their foes in open warfare or man to man, their very timidity impels them to treachery or a violation of the laws of hospitality, when, by long-continued oppression and the loss of relatives, they have been driven to retaliate upon the few individuals or families of the domineering tribe who were living in confidence among them. This remark applies directly to their feud with the Red-knives [Yellowknives], who for many years resorted to the hunting-grounds of the Dog-ribs, tyrannised over them, and carried away their women. This was long borne, but at length, some lives having been lost in the contests which occasionally ensued, the Dog-ribs, watching their opportunity, cut off several leading Red-knives and their families, who, not dreading any thing at the time, were scattered among the Dog-rib encampments. The details of these reprisals give a curious insight into the character of these people. Some of the victims, deprived of the means of resistance, and aware of their intended fate, travelled for a whole day with the hostile party; but the latter required to have their passions roused by altercation before they acquired sufficient boldness to perpetrate the deed, and were finally incited to its commission by the sufferers demanding to be killed at once if their death was intended, for they would go no further. When the husbands and grown men were killed, the Dog-ribs argued that pity impelled them to slaughter also the wives and children, who would be unhappy and perish for want, having lost their means of support.

Surely a casuistry worthy of the most subtle European politician.

These are one hundred-year-old questions and no one can now begin to attach blame, but if we are using history (as we must) to try to understand our present world, then in all honesty we cannot ignore the data which history presents, though it might be suitable to our present purpose to forget them. Racial conflict in arctic Canada is not now all white versus native, and it never has been; such conflict has also been there between native peoples, Dogrib against Yellowknife, Yellowknife against Inuit. The Yellowknife (or Copper) Indians had guided Samuel Hearne to the mouth of the Coppermine fifty years before Franklin, and as Hearne notes in his diary of May 1771,

a great number of Indians entered into a combination with those of my party to accompany to the Copper-mine River; and with no other intent than to murder the Esquimaux, who are understood by the Copper Indians to frequent that river in considerable numbers. . . . I endeavoured as much as possible to persuade them from putting their inhuman design into execution. . . .

Hearne had served as a midshipman in the Royal Navy (which he joined at age eleven) throughout the Seven Years' War, that real first *world* war fought in North America and India as well as in Europe; he knew something about war's inhumanity, but Indian traditional (hereditary?) enmities seem to him, as to most Europeans, merely savage. And the Indians in turn deride him; they understand him no more than he them. He is, they say, "actuated by cowardice." Since he is the only white man in the company, for his own safety he decides he cannot interfere, but the overwhelming emotion with which he describes the massacre at the mouth of the Coppermine, a spot known to this day as Bloody Fall, attests to his true feelings. The Indians attack the sleeping Inuit camp at one o'clock in the morning, July 17, 1771; at that time the arctic night is, of course, bright as day:

In a few seconds the horrible scene commenced; it was shocking beyond description; the poor unhappy victims were surprised in the midst of their sleep, and had neither time nor power to make any resistance; men, women, and children, in all upward of twenty, ran out of their tents stark naked, and endeavoured to make their escape; but the Indians having possession of all the landside, to no place could they fly for shelter. One alternative only remained, that of jumping into the river; but, as none of them attempted it, they all fell a sacrifice to Indian barbarity!

The shrieks and groans of the poor expiring wretches were truly dreadful; and my horror was much increased at seeing a young girl, seemingly about eighteen years of age, killed so near me, that when the first spear was stuck into her side she fell down at my feet, and twisted round my legs, so that it was with difficulty that I could disengage myself from her dying grasps. As two Indian men pursued this unfortunate victim, I solicited very hard for her life; but the murderers made no reply till they had stuck both their spears through her body, and transfixed her to the ground. They then looked me sternly in the face, and began to ridicule me, by asking if I wanted an Esquimaux wife; and paid not the smallest regard to the shrieks and agony of the poor wretch, who was twining round their spears like an eel! Indeed, after receiving much abusive language from them on the occasion, I was at length obliged to desire that they would be more expeditious in dispatching their victim out of her misery, otherwise I should be obliged, out of pity, to assist in the friendly office of putting an end to the existence of a fellow-creature who was so cruelly wounded. On this request being made, one of the Indians hastily drew his spear from the place where it was first lodged, and pierced it through her breast near the heart. The love of life, however, even in this most miserable state, was so predominant, that though this might justly be called the most merciful act that could be done for the poor creature, it seemed to be unwelcome, for though much exhausted by pain and loss of blood, she made several efforts to ward off the friendly[!] blow. My situation and the terror of my mind at beholding this butchery, cannot easily be conceived, much less described; though I summed up all the fortitude I was master of on the occasion, it was with difficulty that I could refrain from tears; and I am confident that my features must have feelingly expressed how sincerely I was affected at the barbarous scene I then witnessed; even at this hour I cannot reflect on the transactions of that horrid day without shedding tears.

Hearne was a very tough, resourceful man; he had just spent two years accomplishing one of the most incredible physical feats in recorded history: walking from Hudson Bay to the Coppermine, in winter and in summer, in light and in darkness. He had without apparent qualm participated in a world war between French and English (do economics and known, accepted *manners* make such organized, planned killing less "savage"?). But the single death of that girl at his feet broke him; as it should have.

I have not quoted this gruesome description to emphasize either a territorial imperative nor Konrad Lorenz's theory on aggression. There was no territorial necessity for this massacre: the Yellowknives had to travel for days over open country with plenty of migratory caribou in it before they reached the falls. And I do not agree with the Lorenzian theory that human beings, like all animals, have an *instinct* to seek and fight (not necessarily kill) a rival of their own kind and that mankind's fatal flaw is that it has developed "artificial" rather than natural weapons and so it lacks the instinctive inhibitions carnivores have against killing their fellows. Nor do I wish here to emphasize the scene's savagery, though Hearne, who has lived through a bit himself, does not hesitate to do that. Certainly the white wars of the time were no different. Slavery still fueled the economy of the Christian world; English sea captains had the legal right to whip a "free" sailor to death for disobedience — as Hugh MacLennan has pointed out with striking effectiveness in his essay "The Shadow of Captain Bligh." Nor need we go back so far in history: our own century has more than we care to consider of similarly planned racial and religious and political savagery, not the least of which is the daily planning by our politicians and generals to devise new ways of incinerating millions of men, women and children with nuclear missiles. We are of course civilized, and so could not countenance destroying our victims as they curled in agony about our legs, but if they can be annihilated at an unseeable distance by dropping napalm from seven miles up or by pressing buttons, we need not thereby disturb even our dinners, leave alone our sleep or our consciences. We simply call that "anticipatory defense."

That world of missiles and bombs and star wars is strikingly close to what we think of as the remote people of the North. They are, after all, the North Americans in closest proximity to the Soviet Union. Many of them have worked on the DEW Line, built to warn us of our imminent incineration. Regularly now the cruise missiles fly from their Beaufort Sea launch down the valley of Mackenzie's river — the terrain, as one might expect, is so similar to the Siberian terrain just on the opposite curve of the North Pole. And the night sky is so clear there, if you glance up, all the satellites and assorted world military snooping machinery are impossible not to see. Three o'clock one August morning as I left the community dance in Paulatuk (meaning "The Place of the Smoking Earth") I saw those heavenly lights which for an instant look just like particularly brilliant stars, but in an instant you notice them moving in relation to all those other marvelously motionless points and you are afraid: you want the heavens above to speak in their eternal, silent immovable way, as they always have to all people throughout history. Dear God, we have infected the very stars with our fears and hatreds.

The Canadian people of the Arctic now live in settled communities; their days of nomadic hunting seem to be over. Except for individual hunters or trappers (trappers whose way of life has been very nearly destroyed by animal rights advocates in Europe), they rarely make long forays onto the land or the sea, depending on the season, which

97

Thrasher talks about. Bruce Chatwin, in a book called *The Songlines* (which are, apparently, labyrinths of sound pathways which stretch to every corner of Australia — but I can't get misled into that here), Chatwin speaks of his fascination for nomads, for his "quest to know the secret of their irreverent and timeless vitality. Why is it," he asks, "that nomad peoples have this amazing capacity to continue under the most adverse circumstances, while the empires come crashing down?"

Chatwin apparently has never been in the Arctic; he has studied the herding nomads of Africa and the Middle East, but a good deal of what he writes could still apply to the Inuit though they are no longer nomads. To fly in August into Paulatuk, to see its short fringe of single road and single line of houses on the inner curve of Darnley Bay, is to come to a community where television, radio, the airplane, electricity, school and post office are as much a part of life as in any other Canadian settlement. But the landscape is utterly different: there is not a shrub higher than your ankle anywhere; the road ends at the nearest lake; the brown two-story houses, prefabricated in southern Canada, stand up baldly in their row, set on posts with their insulated floors exposed to wind which blows under them ceaselessly. If the houses were set on the permafrost of the ground, that peculiar arctic continuation of water pretending to be land *within* the land itself, their weight and warmth would melt it and the building would sag, crash, probably at some point crumple the way they have so picturesquely, for example, in the ancient gold-rush town of Dawson City, Yukon. Buildings like that look intriguing but they are hellish to live in during a long winter. On the one street of Paulatuk two enormous trucks patrol: one pumps water from the lake into the houses, the other pumps out wastes. But this is August and everyone is waiting for the annual barge from Inuvik, the end of the road seven or eight hundred sea and river kilometres away. Perhaps another pick-up truck will arrive then; certainly the store manager has ordered four all-terrain tricycles (the summer equivalent of snowmobiles) and they have already been sold. I hate both such machines; their snarl is even worse than chain saws', but a few hours walking on the tundra convince me of certain elemental facts — but I will return to walking later. August is not for walking; it is the northern month for fishing char.

For though this community is fixed, electrified, dominated by those regulars of southern communities: airline schedules, church, store hours, school, the remnants of its hunting year remain visible everywhere. It is not only in the pile of caribou and muskox bones, antlers, skulls heaped beside some houses, the immense, weathered and ancient vertebra of a bowhead whale beside antlers (parts of it sawed off for carving). No, August is for fishing and freezing fish (in the new flash freezer, not by the traditional storing on ice) as July is for hunting beluga whale and cutting in for muktuk — a delicacy to the Inuit but very much an acquired taste, as I discovered. In fact, trying it frozen — which is, they tell me, best — is as tasty as greasy grasshopper. September is for hunting caribou: they are moving south then, their coats excellent just before the fall rut and the heaviest winter cold make them too heavy, and the early winter for trapping martin, wolverine, white fox along the edge of the treeline. Then comes dark winter, a time for sealing out on the sea ice and the possibility of yourself being hunted by the polar bears who are sealing too. Then comes the quick arctic spring of returning birds until the opening water brings the whales again. All the rituals, the traditional annual rounds are there in vestige still imaged in the methodical movement of the old man in his boat on the pale green sea water: he is going out around the headland to check his nets for char on the Hornaday River. Riding in Edward Ruben's boat with him, I can see a little of what that ancient annual hunter round of landscape and season has become today.

Felix Nuyviak of Tuktoyaktuk has made a moving oral elegy of his memory of the time when that cycle meant life itself. He was born before the turn of the century and like all the old people recorded (some on video) telling the stories of their lives, they all begin: "I remember when my parents were still alive, people live always happy." Or "People used to have lots of fun in them days, no hard times." But Felix Nuyviak, recorded in 1976, takes us through the nomadic year until the Big Flu of 1902 struck the people of the Mackenzie Delta. Here is his story, recorded by Nellie Cournoyea:

From my childhood, I keep all the memories; more importantly, by going to sleep as a boy, I missed a great many tales, legends, and songs. But still I remember, even though I was a young boy, hunting birds with a sling shot and a small ball. Of the most enjoyable times of my childhood and the most treasured now, was at that time, a long time ago, I looked forward to the exciting time of the gathering at Kittigazuit, or Christmas in old days. What a time for the Inuit. Young and old enjoyed it. Every bit of it. [Kittigazuit used to be where the Beaufort Sea and the Mackenzie River join, somewhere. The site is now deserted.]

In those days our ancestors didn't live by a clock. Perhaps only by the big one, the reliable one — the sun. Sukina. Beast of the land, bird of the air, all the fish and whale and seal and all of life as regulated in a cycle. There was a time for working, a time for hunting, fishing and a time also for relaxation, for amusement and entertainment. Entertainment period was on when the sun was lost on the horizon and lasted until it returned in January.

From everywhere, people would arrive in Kittigazuit for the winter festivities. How many could there be? I do not know. I didn't know how to add, how to subtract then. But there were so many at Kitti and the opposite shore in the other village, Kukbak. Whenever they played games on the ice — a kind of soccer or rugby, the water would move and shake in the water holes. At night time, what a fury of light from all snowhouses. Lights generating from a soapstone lamp and illuminating all the snow houses. I liked to look from Kitti to Kukbak at night. These were our Christmas decorations and display of lights. Like now — here with our electric lights.

(It is worth noting that in 1821 when Dr. John Richardson for the first time saw an igloo built, he could not contain his wonder. The Inuit translator, Augustus, built it at Ft. Enterprise and Richardson, after detailing exactly the method of its construction, concluded:

The purity of the material of which the house was framed, the elegance of its construction and the translucency of its walls, which transmitted a very pleasant light gave it an appearance far superior to a marble building and one might survey it with feelings somewhat akin to those produced by the contemplation of a Grecian temple reared by Phidias [the designer of the Parthenon]. Both are triumphs of art inimitable in their kinds.

And both, of course, use those building materials which their particular land offers: in Greece it is stone, in the Arctic snow.)

Felix Nuyviak continues:

Hospitality, kindness, display of generosity were the rule then and our oldest people would invite all to share food and to play and participate in games of various kinds. And competition was keen, challenges taken. Kee kee keooakta neereekta. Day after day was spent watching games, dances, listening to songs and stories, participating in the activities.

There was the game Oahootuktook, game of wrestling, game tugging at someone's arm, the mouth pull etc. And at the end there was a champion. At these endings the Inuit would display the Tumerat, puppets of swans, bear and fox. And it seemed really alive. At the very end of the festivities, before departure and dispersal, at the reappearance of the sun, all ... the oil for the lamp, all old oil was thrown out. New oil was put in lamps and the game of dart

101

shooting started where all participated, putting out bets. This would conclude the time of relaxation.

But all was not fun in those days, the seas were clear also. The Anguat court would give advice and rule to be strictly followed, sometimes successfully, sometimes also without result.

Another period of the year when people got together, and a popular one I should say, is in July. That is the time of whale hunting. But then there was no time for games. It was hard work. This was done at Kitti, at Oookeevik and Adavuglar. No gun was used for whales then, only the harpoons. After chasing the whale in shallow water, a herd of them, when grounded and the water receded, we harpooned them and pursued the wounded ones. Annugua did not return to that place where they hunted the big blue whale, no guns were used: harpoons and whale bone omiak [boat] only. And they always had their own song for hunting.

After whale hunting we parted once more to go fishing in all the surrounding rivers and lakes. It was a time also for some volunteers or delegates to go to the place of the big houses, Fort McPherson, and purchase some articles. Taniktuk we called them — tea, flour, sugar, tobacco and later in time, powder and lead for cartridges. Ooulua [name of a man] could make such a trip and went quite often, to Ft. McPherson.

Then in the autumn it was time for the preparation for winter tools, ooniak, the sleigh, the harnesses were made or repaired in the kasgar, the work house used for workshop and especially the man-meeting place. Only men were allowed there, no children. The women would now and then bring in some food. In those days, staying late at night was unknown. Around 6 p.m. perhaps, a man will return home and around 9 p.m. be ready to retire and sleep. They were early risers, early birds in the morning. And at that time too, children were very respectful to their elders and their parents. Oh, yes sometimes they, being excited, had to be calmed down and if the time were not enough to establish peace and quiet, then an akla, a brown bear, would enter the house with many ha, ha, ha! The brown bear with a head, big eyes and showing big teeth and an open mouth, ready to grab little children. This was more than enough to raise peace and quiet in the house because this was very frightening.

At the very first snowfall, Neenoceea [name of a man] would travel around hunting, sometimes camping, careful not to forget some driftwood so he could find a place to tie the dogs. The harness was made of skins and he tied them right on the pole to prevent the dogs from reaching and eating them. And the sleigh was also turned upside down, as all the pieces of it were tied together by skins. All very good food for hungry dogs. Neenoceea, sleigh runners were smeared with mud and water to give them a very good ability to skid on the snow or ice.

In those days old people were always on the move. The only thing that mattered for them was food. Food of any kind, without having too much rest. There'll be time later for rest, at the very end, at death. The ritual which really marks me is that event that happened in 1902 at Kitti, it is still clear and vivid in my memory. I was there when the flu epidemic destroyed my tribe, countless died, young and old.

The best of our people, the peak, had come to Kitti for the whale hunting [in July]. As only a few were out at their camps, the oldest and most skillful were there whale hunting. The terrible epidemic did not respect the old people's health. Some were there only for a few days, others for a very, very brief period. This was the end of the tribe, the end of Kitti, the end of Kukbak. The place which was filled up with laughter, noise, running, activity, became a land of desolation. Death was everywhere. The younger people that remained tried their best to whale. People no longer went to Kittigazuit; I remember in the evenings when it got dark it was absolutely quiet all over. People seemed afraid to speak. People dying everywhere, so many they had to quit bothering to make graves. At times they would put 2 or 3 bodies together, not in the underground but just where the body was covered by logs, and the tools no longer respectfully arranged in and around the resting place. The women of the tribe left Kitti afraid, frightened at leaving a hounded and forsaken land, a land stricken by evil spirits and a wall of pain lying on the shoreline, but empty now — unattended and abandoned as they were.

I was among those refugees who took shelter in another place to live. Other surroundings — I, Uangu Nuviooaviar. Lest you forget them, remember. And we will remember the tales and sing the songs and recall the feats and virility of our ancestors and yours, men of stature and strength and courage, above all men living in the land, their land, our land now. Where to survive, one must be a human being, etu nuvialu.

I found parts of this great elegy for the Mackenzie Inuit in a number of stories Felix Nuyviak told before his death. Again and again he remembers that dreadful dying, the names of his people and flu against which they had no immunity brought no doubt by the white whalers for whom so many of the people then worked. The whalers took only the baleen (head bone) and the spermaceti (head oil) of the whales — leaving all of the gigantic body for the Inuit. The whalers, as Robin McGrath has pointed out in her excellent introduction to Agnes Nanogak's collection *More Tales from the Igloo*, arrived about 1890; they came from everywhere in the world and they brought prosperity with trade, yes, but also alcohol and disease and in many cases dreadful abuse of all kinds upon the people by taking advantage of their kindly, generous social customs. As in any encounter between an industrialized and a hunting culture, the amount of *stuff*, of *made* things that such a society can by means of endless ships drag into a world of finitely numbered things — a culture that has developed only such articles as can be carried on one's back or, at most, taken from place to place by dogs — the very *stuff* itself of the industrial world overwhelms the indigenous culture. The flu epidemic created a vacuum among the Mackenzie Inuit; there simply were too few people left and so others from the west — Alaskan Inuit — and the north and east — the Copper Inuit of Victoria Island — gravitated toward the rich Mackenzie Delta hunting and trapping territory, for just as the whaling industry failed so the world prices for muskrat and fox rose dramatically. Agnes Nanogak, Holman Island storyteller and artist, was born of the marriage of such a Copper Inuit woman, Topsy Ikiunak, and the Alaskan Eskimo William Natkutsiak, the outstanding hunter who became Vilhjalmur Stefansson's guide and companion in ten years of arctic exploration. Natkutsiak, known now mostly as Billy Banksland, began working with Stefansson in 1908 and he and Topsy, perhaps more than any other people, made possible those prodigious arctic journeys on land and ice which made Stefansson the greatest arctic explorer Canada has ever had.

Stefansson is so fascinating a character that he must be avoided; the whale which is his life would swallow any storyteller — a man who lived a third of his adult life on the ice and tundra of the Arctic and the rest in the artistic community of Greenwich Village, New York. Some commentators say he wrote fine poetry, others insist his immensely popular factual books about his northern travels are impressive fictions. In one sense he was a North popularizer like Farley Mowat, but he was much better trained both as a scientist and a philosopher; nevertheless, one of his first loves was literature: a rare combination for a man who before the age of forty found life in an igloo more interesting than sitting behind a desk. As you can see, his story must be avoided. All I need to explain is that he was born in Manitoba, grew up in North Dakota, and sometimes considered himself a reincarnated Norseman rediscovering the lost Vineland of the North which the sagas narrate with such vividness. He made his discoveries in the most obvious manner possible; it is so obvious one wonders why whites didn't think of it earlier. They probably did, but rejected it on the basis of some silly "civilized" prejudice. Stefansson made the assumption that the Inuit had lived in the Arctic for millenia, they were human beings just like any white and so if one wanted to live in and explore the Arctic, one must live basically like them.

And so he did. Instead of hauling in tons of expensive supplies and killing his hired men carrying it everywhere (the more men you have, the more supplies you must pack: the whole process is self-defeating), he hired two Inuit men and two women: the men to hunt and drive the dog teams (he quickly realized that the only reliable season for arctic travel is winter; anyone walking a mile across a boggy rocky "nigger-headed" tundra, as they call it, will instantly understand that; and three centuries of Englishmen had proven that the summer sea is always at the whim of the ice pack moved where it listeth by the omnipresent wind), the women to cook and keep the hide clothes in order by sewing. The best arctic boots and mitts and clothing are not made of heavy wool, they are made of caribou and seal hide in designs perfected by the Inuit. But any clothing tears on ice, wears out, and Inuit women know better than anyone in the world how to sew it so that the arctic wind cannot squirm inside.

After 1920, Stefansson spent the last forty years of his life writing excellent books that describe both his personal explorations and his massive research into arctic lore. He had an impressive ego, as all explorers must, not at all unsuitable to the extraordinary man he certainly was, and he told wonderful stories. Fortunately we also have some of his stories from the Inuit point of view. Joe Nasugaluaq, a drummer and storyteller from Tuktoyaktuk who from his youth in 1915 kept a daily syllabic diary with details as precise as the numbers of caribou each local hunter killed on a certain day, Nasugaluaq was a good friend of Billy Banksland, Stefansson's chief hunter. In his memoirs (also recorded by Nellie Cournoyea) Nasugaluaq provides many particularities Stefansson does not bother to mention in his writing. For example, he tells us that in 1910 Stefansson was living with one of the Inuit women he had hired, a woman named Pannigabluk or "Fanny" as she was later called. "It was hardly noticeable," says Nasugaluaq, but at the same time any cohabitation would have been impossible to hide in a snowhouse. And why should it be hidden? In the long winter darkness, in a world where life itself can so easily be lost, why should human beings not give each other all the warmth and closeness possible? The Inuit certainly did, and as for Stefansson, why can one only be a true "explorer" if one regularly starves to the point of death? If one suffers every possible privation, including above all the privation of human companionship, warmth and love?

Stefansson didn't think so: he learned to speak Inuktitut fluently and he tried to think like an Inuit and he lived like one; his greatness as an arctic scientist and explorer was rooted in exactly such behavior. Nevertheless, he remained "white" enough to try and maintain all his life a (the most typical?) white arctic secret. In his book, *My Life with the Eskimo* (1913), which describes his second expedition of 1908-12, he frequently mentions Fanny as the cook and marvelously skilled seamstress who kept all their clothing in order. She was with him again when he led the Canadian Arctic Expedition of 1913-18, but he does not mention her name in the eight-hundred-page book he wrote about it, *The Friendly Arctic* (1921); nor does he do so in his posthumously published autobiography, *Discovery* (1964). In fact, not even to one of his closest acquaintances, the arctic writer and traveller Richard Finnie, would he ever acknowledge that he lived with her or that her child was his. Finnie himself, in an article in *North*, attempts to prove that the only descendant Stefansson had (he married Evelyn Baird of New York when he was sixty-two but had no children with her) was a son who lived all his life in the Mackenzie Delta. He was named Alex Stefansson and he died in Aklavik in 1969.

In August 1987, I met Alex's wife Mabel in the Inuvik Hospital; the old lady had a lovely round Inuit face, beautiful half-hooded eyes, high cheekbones. The first thing she said to me was, "They called my husband a bastard!" And she showed me a picture of herself and her husband in a typical bush camp: he was tall, gaunt, blondish; a Viking if ever there was one. "He was a real good hunter," she said, "but easy to get mad. His mother was Fanny Alachuk, he was born in 1910 on Point Parry."

If one uses Stefansson's own chronology in *My Life with the Eskimo*, his party was at Point Parry from March to May 1910; that means he must have been living with Fanny almost immediately when he took her on as a seamstress at Herschel Island in August 1909. He describes her only as "an elderly countrywoman whose husband had died the year before." Nasugaluaq calls her "young." Richard Finnie discovered the following entry in the baptismal register in All Saints Church at Aklavik:

Fanny Pannigabluk, wife of Stefansson, baptized at age of 45 years on August 21, 1915 at Herschel [Island] by [Rev.] C.E. Whittaker.

Alik Alaluk, 5 years old, son of V.S. and Fanny, baptized August 21, 1915 at Herschel by C.E. Whittaker.

On evidence only Fanny could have provided, the Anglican church at least considered Alex Stefansson's son. Nasugaluaq quotes Billy Banksland as saying there were "lots of white children scattered from that first expedition."

In 1961 Georgina Stefansson, then a grade five student at Inuvik Federal School, wrote in *North* magazine: "As the granddaughter of Dr. Vilhjalmur Stefansson, I am naturally very proud of him. Therefore I would like to tell you about him." She goes on to summarize briefly his life's work and concludes:

He married an Eskimo girl, Fannie Puniovaluk; who also helped him in his work. They had only one child, my father, who now lives at Aklavik, where he owns a freighter and hunts and traps in his spare time.

My grandmother died many years ago. Since then my grandfather moved to the United States. He now lives in New York. He still writes many wonderful stories of the north.

Although I have never met him I have always been proud of him, and feel that I do know him because of the stories my dad has told me about him.

Finnie comments: "Evelyn showed Stef the composition which was illustrated with a photograph of him. He glanced at it without a comment." Eventually he did acknowledge to her that Fanny's baby might have been his, but he could not be sure, since, he said, "An Eskimo woman would name her baby after the most important man, or leader, for the sake of status."

A year later, on August 26, 1962, Vilhjalmur Stefansson died in Hanover, New Hampshire, where on the Dartmouth College Green he had often built a winter igloo. No doubt little Georgina never did meet him.

In 1938 Stefansson published a book for whose "central idea" he said, "I am indebted to my old friend Stephen Leacock." It proved to be the most popular book he ever wrote, and it would seem he dedicated it to Fannie Hurst, the American novelist whose lover he had been for seventeen years. As I was looking at the book while writing these sentences, I had a sudden recognition: its title is *Unsolved Mysteries of the Arctic*, and the dedication reads simply: "To FANNIE." But there are, of course, two Fannys. When in the ultimate privacy of his thoughts Stefansson considered his past, and how that second expedition had made him a world-renowned polar expert and determined his entire (I would say magnificent) life's work, which Fanny did he really mean: the New York socialite and writer of passing entertainment or the Inuit helpmeet of his youth and mother of his child? Where did he learn more about human mystery, in Greenwich Village or in an igloo? Unsolvable mystery, secret indeed.

One other Joe Nasugaluaq story about Stefansson's "acculturation" to the North. Food was always a problem, especially for Stefansson who travelled with up to sixty dogs, and one difficult winter he negotiated with a shaman named Payalliq to buy his shaman power for hunting from him "so his dogs could never go hungry." He offers Payalliq a primus stove for his secret, and the shaman agrees:

"Sure, why not, you're the boss. It's up to you." He tells him the song and then he explains how to use it. "If you're going to use the power," he explained, "you have to tie this wood around your mittens or your neighbor's feet and then you sing and ask the Big Boss, sing right and the wood will get really heavy. But if it doesn't get heavy, it won't work." Then Stefansson wanted to try it immediately, but Payalliq said it wouldn't work then because he didn't need it then, he had lots of frozen seals in his caches. So Stefansson gave him the primus stove and the kerosene.

He was going back and forth all winter, going east and he had Pannigabluk then travelling with him and sewing his clothing and Natkutsiaq was with him too, hunting and driving the other dog team. They had over thirty dogs in two teams and when they came to the Smoking Mountains they were running out of dogfeed. "Don't worry," Stefansson told Tanaumiq who was there with the others, "I've got the power, I'm going to perform tonight and we'll shoot plenty of caribou tomorrow, don't worry." So that night he tied the power to his mittens and he was singing and singing but the wood wouldn't get heavy. Nothing whatsoever was happening so finally he had to give it up. He was really mad. "That Payalliq," he said, "he got one of my primus stoves and my dogs are going to starve anyway!" He found out you can't purchase that kind of power for anything, maybe because he himself had been baptized.

Well, I have been baptized too. I am sitting in Edward Ruben's boat at the mouth of the Hornaday River and he and his son James are pulling plenty of dog food (whitefish) out of the water without any apparent song, and also arctic char which is superb food for human beings. I need more than food; I need comprehension. Perhaps, if I have nerve enough to acknowledge it, I need something as venerable as — and I hesitate to say it, such an ancient, old-fashioned "secret" to which one hardly dare confess in the present dark age of irony — I need wisdom. Wisdom to understand why Canadians have so little comprehension of our own *nordicity*, that we are a northern nation and that, until we grasp imaginatively and realize imaginatively in word, song, image and consciousness that North is both the true nature of our world and also our graspable destiny we will always go whoring after the mocking palm trees and beaches of the Caribbean and Florida and Hawaii; will always be wishing ourselves something we aren't, always stand staring south across that mockingly invisible border longing for the leeks and onions of our ancient Egyptian nemesis, the United States. Is climate, is *weather* to be all that determines what we think ourselves to be?

The Rubens, father and son and grandson, wade through the shallow, stormy water dragging their heavy boat. Water slapping at me, I wade after them to the bank where their white tent stands, the only visible shape on the tundra. Two poles hold up the radio wire. They debate a moment whether I should take their rifle in case I meet a grizzly. I can see in all directions to the horizon: where could a grizzly be hiding anywhere there? Before I can mention my antipathy towards guns they decide it is unnecessary, and quickly I agree. If a bear happens along I will have to play dead, though I am not at all sure that is a game I know how to play. Or want to. I thank them and walk south across tundra towards the hills.

It seems you can walk wherever you please; there is not a single scattered erratic or even the lowest brush to decide your track. I am thinking of words to describe why, in a kilometre or two, I am already so tired: spongy/ rocky/ rutted/ exhausting/ endless; all of them seem to apply. Almost an hour and through air sharp as glass — if I lift my hand I can touch it, just there, there — I can still see that white tent, the boat nosed up on the sand wedge of the river — or is it the sea? The boat balanced on the restless line between water and land. I should practise a little, playing dead. Caribou, ptarmigan, ground squirrels, foxes would be easy; muskox perhaps more problematic. The guides in Paulatuk tell me the only problem with taking whites to hunt muskox is to make the trek long and difficult enough to justify the fee; once found they behave more or less like herds of cows: stand motionless and always face you and so there is plenty of time to stand back and consider which has the best set of horns. However, if you for some inadvertent or unwitting reason disturb their circled stance — I can see the small headline in southern newspapers: "Canadian novelist trampled to death by confused muskox on open tundra."

There are no willows anywhere. Perhaps I could run, perhaps I could draw a line with my finger in the earth and water would gush up, so I bend to the tough tussocks I have stumbled over, to the thin moss so tight on the stony earth and a ptarmigan I haven't and wouldn't have seen (is my blindness all around me?) bursts out running at my feet and when I recover my balance and can bend again, two centimetres below the cool surface I feel, abrasive as stone, the deep, deep cold. I tear what surface I can clutch with both hands (a running finger is laughable) and there is the grey, eternal ice, within the very land itself, oozing moisture at the air or my hesitant finger, true, but a century would barely offer a trickle. There is no question about what I will need to do here.

But then I do reach a rise: the horizon does have edges. Below me is the flashing clear blue curve of the Hornaday River where the char are moving towards the indelible place of their birth, their new birthing, and the empty hills rise beyond hills all grey-green in the August sunlight. A landscape like the knobby palm of God's hand. And along the river cliffs I suddenly discover I am walking on trees. Prehistoric trees huge as redwoods. They are petrified cross sections of a forest here before history. I pocket some bits of stone bark: I cannot even lift the fractures of branches, leave alone budge the gnarled red stems of them thrust at me out of the cliffs. Before the unnumbered ages of ices.

Aritha van Herk, the author of that superb northern novel *The Tent Peg* (and the only one as far as I know written by a woman), writes me that I should "find the north in your own head." Where is it? I do not know. But I am moving, and what I encounter here in the North, where I have of necessity come to look, are secrets; enigmas; mysteries. Not mysteries in the fine New Testament sense of a secret once hidden and then inexplicably revealed through the mercy of divine revelation. No, not that; at least not yet. And it was pretentious of me to so quickly conceive of such a title for a series of public lectures: The Arctic, Landscape of the Spirit. Indeed, walking alone in this enormous landscape where I am all eyes and no sight, it is not only surrounding me but the image of it from the air is playing doubled, trebled through every sense of my awareness, I am steadily rendered more and more word-less. One could so easily, perhaps one must of necessity become a motionless dot of stillness. Experience the day and night and moon and sun and the imperceptible turn of the stars.

Nevertheless words will gather, linear as any river growing out of the sea. An epigraph by J. Michael Yates:

> So many of us, alas, were born with
> no Northwest Passage to discover.
> We spend our lives carrying that
> poignant absence inside us wherever
> we go, around and around the earth.

No, I desire true NORTH, not PASSAGE to anywhere. If I must I will accept areal over linear, accept it of myself, bear or no bear. The ice rigid in the land below the moss under my feet, the relentless motion of the sea speaking forever on the rocks as I for an instant passed them and heard: Pablo Neruda in his antarctic Chile, that global, rocky mirror of my arctic Canada, accepted it somehow in his poem "Yo Volvere," translated by Alistair Reid as "I Will Come Back:"

> Some time, man or woman, traveller,
> afterwards, when I am not alive,
> look here, look for me here
> between the stones and the ocean,
> in the light storming in the foam.
> Look here, look for me here,
> for here is where I shall come, saying nothing,
> no voice, no mouth, pure,
> here I shall be again the movement
> of the water, of
> its wild heart,
> here I shall be both lost and found —
> here I shall be perhaps both stone and silence.

Yes. Between the stones and the ocean, a surface so narrow it is no more than a possible line for a possible balance. The few people of this land have always lived on that "between," and they have never been reduced to stillness; they remain living people. They call themselves *Inuk*: a man, pre-eminently. Here and there, very carefully they build inukshuk, the stone figures that declare their presence. And their words inhabit this landscape: I must turn again to those words, three times removed from their original though I am.

And I remember a poem by Orpingalik of the Netsilik Inuit from Pelly Bay on the Simpson-Boothia Peninsulas which created, of course, the last fatal barrier for the English to discover the Northwest Passage through the frozen arctic seas. Rasmussen records the poem, and he tells us that in 1921 Orpingalik was a skillful hunter and leader of the Netsilik, both a powerful shaman and poet. With a succession of wives he had twenty-one children (remarkable considering that the Netsilik at that time in total numbered only 259) and "he was always singing; he called his songs 'comrades in solitude.'" "I cannot tell you how many songs I have," he told Rasmussen. "All my being is song, I sing as I draw breath." In the winter of 1939 a French traveller named Gontron de Poncins met this remarkable man at Pelly Bay; even then he still hunted caribou with bow and arrow, the polar bear with a lance and he was "a rosy-cheeked bright-eyed ancient as round as a ball in his white *kuliktak*, or outer coat. He was the only Eskimo I ever saw who had a full square-cut beard." He was then too crippled to walk, but a black and a white dog attached to a tiny sled pulled him over the sea ice to the *aglu*, the sealing breathing holes. Standing on the tundra I remember one of his first great songs, one he composed during a lengthy illness:

My Breath

I will sing a song,
A song that is strong.
   Unaya — unaya.
Sick I have lain since autumn,
Helpless I lie, as if I were
My own child.

Sad, I would that my woman
Were away to another house,
To a husband
Who can be her refuge
Safe and secure as winter ice.
   Unaya — unaya.

Sad, I would that my woman
Were gone to a better protector,
Now that I lack strength
To rise from my couch.
   Unaya — unaya.

Do you know yourself?
So little you know of yourself.
Feeble I lie here on my bench
And only my memories are strong!
   Unaya — unaya.

Beasts of the hunt! Big Game!
Often I chased the fleeing quarry!
Let me live it again, and remember,
Forgetting my weakness.
   Unaya — unaya.

Let me recall the great white
Polar bear,

High up its white body,
Black snout in the snow, it came!
He really believed
He alone was a male
And ran toward me.
   Unaya — unaya.

He threw me down
Again and again,
Then breathless departed
And lay down to rest,
Hid by a mound on a floe.
Heedless he was, and unknowing
That I was to be his fate.
Deluding himself
That he alone was a male,
And unthinking
That I too was a man!
   Unaya — unaya.

I shall never forget that great blubber-beast,
A fjord seal,
I killed in the sea ice
Early, long before dawn,
While my companions at home
Still lay like the dead,
Faint from failure and hunger,
Sleeping.
With meat and with swelling blubber
I returned so quickly
As if merely running over ice
To view a breathing hole there.
And yet it was
An old and cunning male seal.

But before he had even breathed
My harpoon head was set,
Mortally deep in his neck.

That was my way then.
Now I lie feeble on my bench
Unable to get even a little blubber
For my wife's stone lamp.
The time, the time will not pass,
While dawn gives place to dawn
And spring is upon the village.
   Unaya — unaya.

But how long will I lie here?
How long?
And how long must she go begging
For fat for her lamp,
For skins for clothing
And meat for a meal?
A helpless thing — a defenceless woman.
   Unaya — unaya.

Do you know yourself?
So little you know of yourself!
While dawn gives place to dawn,
And spring is upon the village.
   Unaya — unaya.

Ahh, to breathe like that.

    It seemed to me then, motionless on the green, icy land bordered everywhere by water, that certain things might be possible for me. Perhaps eventually the mercy would be given me to encounter what Orpingalik explained to Rasmussen seventy years ago:

Songs are thoughts sung out with the breath when people are moved by great forces and ordinary speech is no longer enough.

A person is moved just like the ice floe sailing here and there out in the current. Your thoughts are driven by a flowing force when you feel joy, when you feel fear, when you feel sorrow. Thoughts can wash over you like a flood, making your breath come in gasps and your heart pound. Something like an abatement in the weather will keep you thawed up. And then it will happen that we, who always think we are small, will feel even smaller. And we will fear to use words. But it will happen that the words we need will come of themselves. When the words we want shoot up of themselves — then we get a new song.

So, I am trying to understand and accept that, and to prepare myself. To walk into the true north of my own head between the stones and the ocean. If I do, I will get a new song. If I do, I will sing it for you.

A SELECTED BIBLIOGRAPHY

Back, George. *Narrative of the Arctic Land Expedition to the Mouth of the Great Fish River, and along the shores of the Arctic Ocean in the years 1833, 1834, and 1835*. London: John Murray, 1836.

Bellot, Joseph René. *Memoirs*. 2 vols. London: Hurst and Blackett, 1855.

Best, George. *The Three Voyages of Martin Frobisher / In search of a Passage to Cathay and India by the North-West, A.D. 1576-8*. Edited with annotations by Vilhjalmur Stefansson. London: Argonaut Press, 1938.

Chatwin, Bruce. *The Songlines*. Markham: Penguin Books, 1987.

Chekhov, Anton. "The Lady with the Pet Dog." In *The Portable Chekhov*. Edited and translated by Avrahm Yarmolinsky. New York: Viking, 1975.

de Poncins, Gontran. *Kabloona*. In collaboration with Lewis Galantiere. New York: Reynal and Hitchcock, 1941.

Dickason, Olive Patricia. *The Myth of the Savage*. Edmonton: University of Alberta Press, 1984.

Finnie, Richard S. "Stefansson as I knew him." *North*, May/June and July/August, 1978.

Franklin, John. *Narrative of a Journey to the Shores of the Polar Sea in the Years 1819-20-21-22*. London: John Murray, 1823.

_____.*Narrative of a Second Expedition to the Shores of the Polar Sea in the years 1825, 1826, and 1827*. London: John Murray, 1828.

Freuchen, Peter. *Peter Freuchen's Book of the Eskimos*. Editor Dagmar Freuchen. New York: World Publishing, 1961.

Gagné, Raymond C. "Spatial Concepts in the Eskimo Language." In *Eskimo of the Canadian Arctic*. Edited by Victor F. Valentine and Frank G. Vallee. The Carleton Library, No. 41. Toronto: McClelland and Stewart, 1968.

Gedalof [McGrath], Robin, editor. *Paper Stays Put: A Collection of Inuit Writing*. Edmonton: Hurtig, 1980.

Grinnell, George. *Blackfoot Lodge Tales*. New York: Scribner, 1921.

Hearne, Samuel. *A Journey from Prince of Wales's Fort in Hudson's Bay to the Northern Ocean in the years 1769, 1770, 1771 & 1772*. London: Strahan and Cadell, 1795.

Hood, Robert. *To the Arctic by Canoe, 1819 - 1821 / The Journal and Paintings of Robert Hood*. Editor C. Stuart Houston. Montreal and London: McGill-Queen's University Press, 1974.

Jenness, Diamond. *Report of the Canadian Arctic Expedition, 1913-18, Volume XIII, Part A: Eskimo Folklore*. Ottawa: The King's Printer, 1924.

_____ and Helen Roberts. *Report of the Canadian Arctic Expedition, 1913-18*,

Volume XIV: Eskimo Songs. Ottawa: The King's Printer, 1925.

King, Richard. *Narrative of a Journey to the Shores of the Arctic Ocean, in 1833, 1834 and 1835*. 2 vols. London: Richard Bentley, 1836.

Kroetsch, Robert. *But We Are Exiles*. Toronto: Macmillan, 1965.

Mackenzie, Alexander. *Voyages from Montreal, on the River St. Lawrence, through the Continent of North America, to the Frozen and Pacific Oceans. In the Years 1789 and 1793*. London: Cadell, 1801.

MacLaren, I.S. "John Franklin." In *Profiles in Canadian Literature, Volume 5*. Editor Jeffrey Heath. Toronto and Reading: Dundurn Press, 1986.

MacLennan, Hugh. *Seven Rivers of Canada*. Toronto: Macmillan, 1961.

———. *Thirty and Three*. Toronto: Macmillan, 1954.

M'Clintock, Francis. *The Voyage of the 'Fox' in the Arctic Seas. A Narrative of the Discovery of the Fate of Sir John Franklin and his Companions*. London: John Murray, 1859.

McGrath, Robin. *Canadian Inuit Literature: The Development of a Tradition*. Canadian Ethnology Service Paper No. 94. Ottawa: National Museum of Man, 1984.

McIlraith, John. *Life of Sir John Richardson*. London: Longmans, Green, 1868.

Nanogak, Agnes. *More Tales from the Igloo*. Introduction by Robin Gedalof McGrath. Edmonton: Hurtig, 1986.

Nansen, Fridtjof. *Farthest North / Being the Record of a Voyage of Exploration of the Ship "Fram" 1893-96*. 2 vols. London: Constable and Co., 1897.

Nasugaluaq, Joe. "Memories." Ms. at Inuvaluit Regional Corp., Inuvik, N.W.T.

Neruda, Pablo. *Las piedras de Chile*. Buenos Aires: Losada, 1961.

North, Dick. *The Mad Trapper of Rat River*. Toronto: Macmillan, 1972.

Nuyviak, Felix. "A Long Time Ago / Memories." Recorded by and translated for Nellie Cournoyea. Ms. at Inuvaluit Regional Corp., Inuvik, N.W.T.

Ohokto. "Ross Meets the Netchiliks." In *Paper Stays Put*. Editor Robin Gedalof [McGrath]. Edmonton: Hurtig, 1980.

Pitseolak, Peter. *People From Our Side*. Editor Dorothy Eber. Edmonton: Hurtig, 1975.

Rasmussen, Knud. *Across Arctic America: Narrative of the Fifth Thule Expedition*. New York: G.P. Putnam's Sons, 1927.

———. *The Netsilik Eskimos: Social Life and Spiritual Culture*. Translator W.E. Calvert. Copenhagen: Gyldendal, 1931; reprinted New York: AMS Press, 1976.

Richardson, John. *Arctic Ordeal / The Journal of John Richardson, 1820-1822*. Editor C. Stuart Houston. Kingston and Montreal: McGill-Queen's University Press, 1984.

———. *Arctic Searching Expedition: A Journal of a Boat-Voyage through Rupert's Land and the Arctic Sea, in seach of the Discovery Ships under Command of Sir*

John Franklin. 2 vol. London: Longman, Brown, Green and Longmans, 1851.

Stefansson, Georgina. "My Grandfather, Dr. Vihjalmur Stefansson." In *North*, July/August, 1961.

Stefansson, Vilhjalmur. *The Friendly Arctic*. New York: Macmillan, 1921.

———. *My life with the Eskimo*. New York: Macmillan, 1913.

———. *Unsolved Mysteries of the Arctic*. New York: Macmillan, 1938; reprinted New York: Collier, 1962.

Thrasher, Anthony Apakark. *Thrasher . . . Skid Row Eskimo*. Toronto: Griffin House, 1976.

van Herk, Aritha. *The Tent Peg*. Toronto: McClelland and Stewart, 1981.

Wallace, Hugh. "Geographical Explorations in 1880." In *A Century of Canada's Arctic Islands*. Editor Morris Zaslow. Ottawa: The Royal Society of Canada, 1981.

Wiebe, Rudy. *The Temptations of Big Bear*. Toronto: McClelland and Stewart, 1973.

———. *The Mad Trapper*. Toronto: McClelland and Stewart, 1980.

Yates, J. Michael. "The Sinking of the Northwest Passage." *Event*, Vol. 1, No. 3, 1972.

Rudy Wiebe was born near Fairholme, Saskatchewan, in 1934 and now lives in Edmonton where he teaches Canadian literature and creative writing at the University of Alberta. Many of his works deal with the people and history of western Canada. In 1973 he was awarded the Governor General's Award for fiction for *The Temptations of Big Bear*. He is also the winner of the Lorne Pierce Gold Medal of the Royal Society of Canada for his contribution to Canadian literature (1987). Wiebe has served as chairman of both the Writers' Guild of Alberta and the Writers' Union of Canada.

Harry Savage